YOUR TOTAL BODY TRANSFORMATION GUIDE!

NEW BODY PLAN

Lose fat and add muscle in just eight weeks!

BY JON LIPSEY

Editorial Director	**Joe Warner**
Photography Director	**Glen Burrows**
Managing Editor	**Chris Miller**
Designer	**Ian Ferguson**
Additional Photography	**Lena Drapella, iStock**

Workouts shot at DW Fitness First. Visit dwfitnessfirst.com for more information.

NEW BODY PLAN ISBN **978-1-9998728-1-6**

CONTENTS

INTRODUCTION	BLOCK 1 / WEEKS 1-2	BLOCK 2 / WEEKS 3-4
006	**040**	**064**

Find out what spurred Jon Lipsey to build his best ever body, and how to start your own transformation

Building some solid strength foundations is the focus of the first fortnight to start the plan on the strongest footing

Adding serious muscular size is the key aim in this block as you start making even bigger changes to your body

BLOCK 3 / WEEKS 5-6

088

Increasing how quickly your body burns fat is the priority in this block, while still adding lean muscle mass

BLOCK 4 / WEEKS 7-8

112

The final block focuses on accelerating the rate of fat loss while adding the finishing touches to your physique

NUTRITION

136

What and when you eat is as important to transforming your body as how you train. Here's all you need to know

New Body Plan
author Jon Lipsey
lost 10kg of fat in
just eight weeks

IF I CAN DO IT, SO CAN YOU

I always doubted my ability to complete a successful body transformation.
Then I gave it a go and got a better result than I ever thought possible

The last eight weeks have changed my life. I'm writing this introduction on the morning of my book cover shoot. That's not a sentence I'd ever thought I'd write. I've been a journalist and editor for 15 years and for my entire career I've been behind the camera. Now it's my turn to sit in the make-up artist's chair, to walk onto the set and, at 37 years of age, turn towards the lights and have my picture taken. I'm nervous, of course, but I'm proud too. I'm proud of what I have achieved in the past two months. I'm proud of going from overweight to being the owner of a cover model body. I've done what I used to tell myself I couldn't do. And if I can do it, you can do it.

NEW BODY, NEW YOU

I don't say that lightly. I say it because I understand what it feels like to not be happy with your body shape. I understand what it feels like to doubt whether you have what it takes to make a big difference in a short space of time. I also, sadly, understand the fear of failure. But now I also know what it feels like to go through a transformation challenge experience and I know that if you make a commitment to start and you give it your best shot, you'll be rewarded in ways you didn't think were possible.

On the surface you'll notice that I have completely changed my body shape. I look healthier and I look younger. What you can't see is that my strength has shot up, my fitness has gone through the roof, I'm sleeping better, I'm less stressed and I have more energy. I also feel in control, like I can do anything I put my mind to, and I'd love for you to experience that too.

EVERYMAN PLAN

I created this plan to answer the simple question – what's the quickest and easiest way to get in shape? I also assumed that you don't have a personal trainer or a fancy meal-prep company. So this book is an everyman guide to getting a cover model body. It lasts for eight weeks because, realistically, that's the shortest timeframe you can give yourself to make the kind of changes you're looking for.

The plan is a gym-based programme that includes four resistance training sessions a week – it's the one I used to transform my own body.

Of course, you can't get in shape if you don't sort out your diet so we've also included detailed information about how to eat to fuel your transformation. It's simpler (and tastier) than you might think, and you'll find all the information you need in the food section that starts on p136.

Finally, I've gone into a bit more detail about my own story over the following pages, to give you an insight into the whole transformation journey. I've also shared my ten secrets of a successful body transformation, and 50 more bits of valuable advice that I picked up along the way.

If I could give one bit of advice to anyone thinking about doing the plan it would be this: start the process, believe in yourself and trust in the plan. Oh, and accept that you'll find it harder to find shirts that fit. Good luck!

Jon Lipsey

FROM LARDY TO LEAN IN 8 WEEKS

I lost 10kg of fat in just eight weeks and transformed my body into cover model material. Here's how it happened – and how you can emulate my results

My name is Jon Lipsey, editor-in-chief of *Men's Fitness* magazine and I have a six-pack. That's not very surprising, is it? You'd expect me to be the proud/smug owner of chiselled abs. In fact, you'd be disappointed if I didn't have a washboard stomach. It's just as well, then, that you didn't meet me eight weeks before I write this because, oh boy, would you have been unimpressed.

You see, two months ago, I didn't have a six-pack. I didn't have T-shirt-filling biceps and I didn't have broad shoulders. I did, however, have a belly. I had love handles too. And big, dark, sleep-deprived circles around my eyes. I was stressed, I had low energy levels and, according to any metric you care to choose, I was overweight.

That's not something I ever thought I'd write. In my mind, weight issues were always someone else's problem. In my teens I was skinny, in my 20s I was slim and I floated into my 30s weighing a svelte 69kg at 1.75m (5ft 9in) tall. Then ,as my responsibilities grew – I started my own business five years ago and I'm due to become a dad for the first time later this year

– so too did my waistline. At 37 years of age, I weighed 80.5kg. Sure, scale weight isn't the only indicator of health, but I doubt that my lengthy training break added over 10kg of muscle mass.

I could tell you that I got a bit "soft around the edges" but the truth is that I got fat. I ate too much, I said "Fancy a swift one?" too often and I moved too little. It didn't happen overnight. It never does. And that's one of the reasons doing anything about it becomes so difficult. What I had to accept, however, was that if my weight gain continued at the same rate then in another seven years, when my child would be wanting to run around in the park, I'd be flirting with a BMI of 30 and about to join the 27% of the British public who, according to 2017 figures, are classed as clinically obese.

I didn't want that to happen, and I desperately wanted to do something about it. There was just one problem. I was absolutely terrified.

REASON TO BE FEARFUL
Even though I work for a fitness magazine, the thought of doing a body transformation has always

WEEK 1

WEEK 8

scared me. I was scared that I wouldn't be able to stick to the diet and exercise plan and I was scared that, even if I did stick to it, I wouldn't get much of a result. I worried that I'd either spend more time in a bar than lifting one, or that my before and after shots would look like a spot-the-difference competition. The final, and perhaps biggest, challenge was that if I failed to make a significant difference to my body shape I'd be exposed as a fraud. Someone who talks a good fitness game but, when it comes to the abdominal crunch, can't put their muscle where their mouth is.

Because of that, it was always easier to pretend that it wasn't happening, to suck in my belly for photographs and to let my fears win. The thing is, I didn't want my kid to have a coward for a dad, so there was really only one option. It was time to put my body and reputation on the line.

The personal goal was to transform my own physique but the broader ambition was to give you, the reader, a plan that would live up to its cover-line claims. I wanted to create an accessible programme that would be the simplest and fastest way to get in shape. So I established a couple of simple rules to make my experience as close as it could be to the one you'll have if you want to do the same thing. I decided that I wouldn't employ a personal trainer and I wouldn't use a fancy meal-preparation service. It would just be me, the weights and an unswerving determination to steer clear of the ice-cream aisle in the supermarket.

The regime I created consisted of four gym sessions a week within a programme composed of four two-week blocks and a nutrition plan that was big on high-quality protein and veg without cutting out any major food groups or making any food forbidden. So beer and crisps aren't strictly banned on this plan, but you consume them in the knowledge that they'll hinder rather than help your progress.

The other significant concept was to gradually ramp up the intensity of the training and the strictness of the diet. Jumping in at the deep end would have been overwhelming and it's important to realise that navigating your way through a transformation challenge is a skill. As your fitness and commitment develop, so too do the demands of the plan.

HOLDING BACK THE BEERS

Once you commit to starting the programme the first week is relatively easy. You're motivated by the promise of what's to come, so you attack the sessions in the firm belief that you're on the path to a brand new body. The nutrition requirements are also manageable – I didn't have to survive on seeds and lettuce leaves. Instead, the first major change was to ditch alcohol. The reason was pretty compelling. Just two pints of lager contains about 400 calories so if you're trying to use up more energy than you're taking in, ice-cold pints become (slightly) less appealing.

Taking shape – how my body changed during the plan

Nobody knows how their transformation will go but you can be sure of two things. One is that progress won't be even. Some weeks will be better than others. Just be patient and you'll be pleased with the outcome. The other is that you'll end up looking in the mirror more often than is helpful. You'll find it more useful to take weekly or fortnightly progress shots like these. Seeing these changes will provide extra motivation.

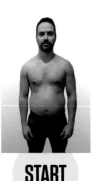

START
Weight **80.5kg**

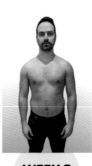

WEEK 2
Weight **77.8kg**

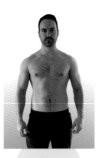

WEEK 4
Weight **75.7kg**

WEEK 6
Weight **73.4kg**

WEEK 8
Weight **71.8kg**

The challenge comes when you realise that Britain is unsteadily propped up by alcohol. We use it to celebrate, to commiserate, to de-stress, to mark the end of another week. It's the lubricant that oils our social wheels. When I met friends for lunch at the end of my first week on the plan, I found a glass of champagne waiting for me on the table. They'd ordered it because they heard I was about to become a dad for the first time. It felt like it would be unfriendly to turn it down so I drank it. A week later I found myself, wine glass in hand, at a relative's 40th birthday celebration. I could have toasted with a sparking water there too but I guess I didn't want to. Ultimately you'll have choices to make during your transformation journey. One glass really won't make a difference but one a week might, so at some point you have to ask yourself which you want more – the booze or the body.

On the plus side, by the end of the first training block I was already seeing positive

High-intensity exercises such as battle rope slams will torch body fat

changes. I was looking less bloated and I even managed to squeeze into a new belt hole. I also discovered that yogurt and sliced frozen banana offers a passable alternative to ice cream (no, honestly). Perhaps this transformation lark was going to be a flourless cake walk after all.

FOOD FIGHT
In the second fortnight of the plan the training schedule changes from an initial upper-body and lower-body split to one that focuses on antagonistic supersets, where you do two exercises back to back that target opposing muscle groups, such as your biceps and triceps. It was tough but effective, and I felt stronger and looked more muscular. My colleague Joe was joining me for a lot of the sessions and that also had a positive impact. If you can find a training partner, their presence will spur you on. You can encourage each other and, if they other guy has just completed a

> "The personal goal for this project was to transform my own physique but the broader ambition was to give you a plan that would live up to its cover-line claim"

set, you're less likely to duck out of the final couple of reps when your turn comes.

The diet, on the other hand, was a little trickier. I discovered during weeks three and four that my blood sugar and hunger hormone regulation was, er, sub-optimal. Before starting the plan I'd never really paid much attention to what I ate. I kidded myself that because I consumed lots of meat, fish, eggs, vegetables and fruit that my diet was fine. The problem is that I really did eat a lot. And I topped it up with stuff that's less nutritionally glorious. I also had an aversion to hunger, which meant that as soon as I wasn't completely full I had a tendency to open the fridge door. I realised that I used fruit to manage my constantly yo-yoing blood sugar levels and, as a result, if I went for any length of time without eating (I'm talking three hours here rather than half a day) I felt terrible. I was also incapable of going for a few hours without a carbohydrate fix.

When I tried to eat in a different way, my brain and body were overtaken by the spirit of an unruly toddler – throwing tantrums when it didn't immediately get what it wanted. I felt fuzzy-headed and I struggled to concentrate. By the time I got to week four the easy fat-loss wins had expired and, although I had made more progress, I didn't feel half way to becoming a cover model.

My only consolation was that at the right angle, in some very forgiving lighting, you could just about see some abs. Well, one ab, really. Only the top right one was brave enough to poke its head above the lardy parapet.

The New Body Plan takes a progressive approach so that as you become fitter the exercises get more demanding

Jon's transformation was so successful it earned him a *Men's Fitness* magazine cover

"The before and after shots capture the physical change I made to my body. What they don't show you is that I transformed my life too. I did what I thought was impossible and, if I can do it, you can too"

FINISHER TOUCH

I went into block three feeling under pressure and behind schedule. The weight was coming off. Just not as fast as I'd like. Thankfully, the plan had a solution. I started to do "finisher" exercises, which are high-intensity interval training moves, such as sled drags and battle rope slams, designed to torch calories and accelerate fat loss. They're highly effective which, in training terms, means they're tough. After my first finisher – ten reps of a 20m prowler push – I slumped on the gym floor, breathing heavily and trying not to reacquaint myself with that morning's breakfast of eggs and vegetables.

After I staggered out of the gym, life tried to trip me up. I had two days of meetings at a trade fair, which meant healthy eating was difficult and training time was under pressure. Then I was off to Germany for another expo, getting up at four in the morning to catch a flight and returning at the end of the day. Unfortunately, my flight back was delayed by over four hours so we didn't take off until after 1.30am. I crawled into bed just as the birds were finding their singing voices and my throat felt like it was on fire. I was ill for the rest of the week, which meant no training and endless cravings for simple carbs.

I faced a decision: force myself to the gym and risk making myself feel worse, or take a couple of rest days and hope that would be enough time to recover. I opted for the latter and it seemed to do the trick. Determined not to let that mini-setback derail my plans, I stepped up my work rate and tried to claw back lost gains. The intention was great but the outcome was not – during an aggressive flye set in week six I suffered a minor pec strain. I could still do chest exercises but I had to hold back, making it almost impossible to build new muscle.

Thankfully the niggle coincided with me outgrowing that toddler response to the new nutrition regime. My body had adapted and it was less carb-reliant. My energy levels were up, my work capacity improved and I embraced the idea that I had two weeks to make sure that I finished the plan with no regrets.

BODY OF EVIDENCE

One of the happy things I can report about doing a transformation challenge is that it gets progressively easier. The second half is easier than the first and the final fortnight is the easiest of all. You're fitter, you're focused and your body has adapted to your new way of eating. I no longer felt exhausted in the evenings and I was sleeping soundly, waking up naturally and energised at 6am. I was getting compliments too. People who hadn't seen me for a few weeks noticed that I looked leaner and healthier. Even personal trainers at the gym I was using were asking me about my workout plan.

The end was in sight and I was training harder than ever but, unexpectedly, it felt great. I felt great. During the final week it seemed like every day made a noticeable difference to how I looked and, for the first time since the project started, I felt like I was going to get the result I was hoping for.

The shoot for the book was arranged for the final day of the plan and when it came around I didn't hit my expectations – I smashed them. The result was better than I could ever have imagined. When I looked in the mirror I couldn't quite believe what I was seeing. When the images started to feed through from camera to computer in the photography studio, it felt like I was looking at someone else's body.

The before and after shots you've seen capture the physical change I made to my body. What they don't show you is that I transformed my life too. I feel ten years younger. I'm energised. I'm calm. I'm happy. I've achieved more than I thought possible in the last eight weeks and I feel like if I can do this, I can do anything. I did what I thought was impossible and, if I can do it, I assure you that you can too.

My only regret? That I didn't do it ages ago.

HOW THE TRAINING PLAN WORKS

Your New Body Plan training programme has been designed to help you build lean muscle mass while also stripping away body fat, especially around your belly. In short, it's an eight-week plan that's going to make you look and feel better than ever!

You can find the full workout plan, including everything you need to know to follow it perfectly, starting on p40. But first, turn the page to get an overview of the theory behind the plan – including how the eight-week plan is split into four two-week workout "blocks", each with its own specific goal – and find out why this approach is the very best method to help you build a bigger, stronger and leaner body in just two months.

The plan is based on resistance training – the best approach to burn fat and build muscle

BLOCK 1

WEEKS 1 & 2

OBJECTIVE GET STRONG

SPLIT UPPER BODY / LOWER BODY / UPPER BODY / LOWER BODY

WHAT In this first workout block the goal is simple: to help you build solid foundations from which you can start to build a bigger and leaner body. So all eight sessions in this block are designed to make you stronger and better at lifting weights, while also adding new lean muscle mass to your frame and starting to chip away at your excess body fat stores to kick-start your body transformation challenge.

HOW You'll do two upper-body and two lower-body sessions each week. Every workout has six exercises, which you'll perform as straight sets. This means that you'll do all the sets and reps of exercise 1, sticking to the tempo and rest periods detailed, and then move on to exercise 2, and so on. This approach is simple to execute and the smartest way to increase strength levels.

BLOCK 2

WEEKS 3 & 4

OBJECTIVE GET BIG

SPLIT CHEST & BACK / LEGS & ABS / BICEPS & TRICEPS / SHOULDERS & ABS

WHAT Now that you're stronger, in this block the workout focus shifts to adding as much lean muscle mass as possible. Doing this, while continuing to burn away your body fat stores – especially around your stomach – will make a big difference to your progress towards building a bigger, stronger and leaner body.

HOW The big change from the previous block is moving from an upper- and lower-body training split to one focusing on individual body parts. This means that each week you'll train, in order, your chest and back; legs and abs; biceps and triceps; and shoulders and abs. This increase in training time dedicated to hitting specific muscle groups will mean you start adding lean muscle mass quickly. This block also introduces supersets to your sessions – these are explained at the start of the chapter.

BLOCK 3

WEEKS 5 & 6

OBJECTIVE GET LEAN

SPLIT CHEST & TRICEPS / LEGS & ABS /
BACK & BICEPS / SHOULDERS & ABS

WHAT The primary goal in this block is to accelerate the speed at which your body burns fat. Having spent the first block getting stronger, and the second block getting bigger, you'll now focus on increasing your body's fat-burning capabilities to move you a huge step closer to achieving that bigger, stronger and leaner physique you want.

HOW To burn body fat faster, at the end of each session in this block you'll do a "finisher", which is a high-intensity interval training (HIIT) drill to send your heart rate soaring and dramatically increase calorie expenditure. The body-part splits have also been changed to keep your body building new muscle effectively. In order, you'll work your chest and triceps; legs and abs; back and biceps; and shoulders and abs.

BLOCK 4

WEEKS 7 & 8

OBJECTIVE GET RIPPED

SPLIT CHEST / BACK & ABS /
BICEPS & TRICEPS / SHOULDERS & ABS

WHAT The focus for the final block of the training programme is to build even more lean muscle mass while stripping away as much fat as possible. You'll already be looking and feeling great, so now's the time to change things up again to work your muscles, heart and lungs even more effectively so that you keep progressing.

HOW To end your New Body Plan looking and feeling bigger, stronger and leaner than you ever thought possible, the workout splits have again been changed. There's a tougher "finisher" at the end of each session to work your legs and abs hard, and to get – and keep – your heart rate high and work up a real sweat, because that's what's going to burn off that last bit of body fat.

HOW THE NUTRITION PLAN WORKS

When you're trying to build a bigger, stronger and leaner body, what you do in the gym has a huge impact on how successful you are. As you have read on the previous pages, the New Body Plan training programme has been specifically designed to test your muscles, heart and lungs hard in a smart and effective way so that your body has no choice but to relinquish existing fat stores and start building lean muscle. But no-one ever built a better body through training alone, and what you eat has as much of an impact on your better-body aspirations as your training.

The nutrition chapter of this programme begins on p136, but turn the page for an overview of the plan's unique approach to eating and nutrition – including why you don't need to count calories or weigh food, or even give up the foods you love, in the pursuit of looking and feeling better than ever.

High-quality protein is a priority if you want to make a radical change to your body shape

FLEXIBLE EATING

WHAT IS IT? The New Body Plan 90% Nutrition method means you eat for a bigger and stronger body 90% of the time – which means eating a variety of healthy, natural and unprocessed sources of carbohydrates, proteins and fats – while still eating for pure pleasure 10% of the time, including all your favourite foods that would be banned on many restrictive and unsustainable diet plans. Because it doesn't ban treats or snacks entirely, you can still eat the foods you love occasionally and build your best ever body.

HOW IT WORKS The beauty of the 90% Nutrition rule is twofold: it's incredibly simple to understand and follow, and it's also incredibly effective in both helping you burn body fat while also building new muscle mass. There's no calorie counting, weighing your food or giving up your favourite treats – all you have to do is eat a balanced and varied diet 90% of the time to build the body you want.

PERFECT PORTION

WHAT IS IT? The Perfect Portion approach is your simple and effective way to make sure you are eating all the essential nutrients you need at every single meal, and therefore giving your body everything it needs to burn fat and build muscle quickly and effectively.

HOW IT WORKS How much you need to eat per meal, and how much of which food groups, will depend on whether your primary goal is to burn body fat or to build muscle. But the simplicity of the Perfect Portion approach is that for either goal, all you need to determine how much food you eat are your hands! We'll explain everything in detail from p152, but for now all you need to know is that every meal needs to contain at least one palm-sized portion of protein, one fist-sized portion of veg, one cupped-hand portion of carbs and a thumb-sized serving of natural fats. There's no need for you to use scales, calculators or apps to build a bigger and leaner body!

FAT LOSS MEAL PLAN

WHAT IS IT? The Flexible Eating method and Perfect Portion approach have been designed to help your burn body fat without having to follow a strict diet plan, so you have complete freedom to base most of your meals around the delicious and nutritious foods you love. But sometimes it can be really helpful – especially when first starting your New Body Plan journey – to have a set of goal-focused meal plans to follow so you can hit the ground running and start torching fat straight away.

HOW IT WORKS The fat-loss meal guide in this plan, which you can find on p158, follow the Perfect Portion approach of using your hands to determine the amount of protein, vegetables, carbs and fat you eat. However, the servings of carbs and fats have been reduced, lowering your overall calorie intake per meal and per day so that your body starts tapping into existing fat stores to release the energy for use as fuel. The protein and veg servings aren't reduced, though, so you'll still give your body the nutrients it needs to build muscle and perform optimally.

MUSCLE MEAL PLAN

WHAT IS IT? Just as the fat-loss meal plans have been tailored to accelerate the burning of body fat for fuel by tweaking the amount of carbs and fats that make up each meal, the muscle-building meal plans (which you can find on p159) have been specifically designed to feed your body more of the essential nutrients it needs to pack on lean muscle mass quickly and efficiently. They also ensure you don't consume more calories than you need so you still tap into existing fat stores for fuel.

HOW IT WORKS The muscle-building meal plans contain more calories, especially from protein, veg and fats, because you need to eat more of these to fuel the process of building lean muscle tissue. There are also more carbohydrates than in the fat-loss meal plans because to build muscle as quickly as possible, you need more carbs to fuel both your workouts and your everyday life. Eating more carbs allows more of the protein you consume to be used for repairing damaged muscle tissues and rebuilding them bigger and stronger.

10 SECRETS OF A SUCCESSFUL TRANSFORMATION

Sleep, dedication, visualisation and more ways to transform how you look and feel fast

THINK LIKE AN ATHLETE

Most people fail to achieve their goals because they struggle to stick to their plan. Simply lasting the distance will massively increase your chances of success. One of the best ways of doing this is to adopt the mindset of an elite athlete.

MAKE IT WORK

If you want to stay motivated then think of your training plan (which will last eight weeks if you follow the New Body Plan) as a training camp in the build-up to a big fight. If you imagine that you're going to step into a ring in front of a huge crowd in a few weeks' time, you're less likely to skip a session. The best bit? In this instance you won't even get hit in the face at the end of it.

APPROACH IT PROGRESSIVELY

If you dive in at the deep end your hopes of a successful transformation may sink without trace. You'll stack the odds in your favour if you gradually increase the intensity and the demands of your training and nutrition plan as you progress.

MAKE IT WORK

Undertaking a successful body transformation is a skill. And as with all new skills, you need to develop your ability gradually. That's why the workouts in this plan have been set at a level that provides a challenge but isn't so tough that it's immediately demoralising. The closer you get to the finish line, the easier it is to push yourself.

THINK IN BLOCKS

Breaking your transformation down into manageable chunks will make it easier to stay motivated. Eight weeks can seem like a long time and it's natural that you'll have doubts about your ability to achieve the result that you want.

MAKE IT WORK

Seeing the eight week period as four two-week blocks gives you a series of achievable goals and allows you to tick off wins as you progress. Within those blocks, you can have mini goals for each week. You should even think of each session as a micro-target. Every one you tick off puts you a step closer to the overall goal. And if you make consistent progress, we guarantee that you'll achieve your overall objective.

ANTICIPATE OBSTACLES

The reality is that your progress is unlikely to be straightforward. You may catch a cold, tweak a muscle or have to deal with something tricky that life throws at you. If you're prepared for that to happen, you can deal with the challenge as it arises.

MAKE IT WORK

Before you start, make a list of the most likely things that could occur and have an adverse effect on your progress. Then write down two or three bullet points about what you'll do should they arise. If something comes up that isn't on the list, simply take a few minutes to write down a list of the things that you can do that are in your control and follow them through until you're able to get back on track.

Take your transformation seriously and you'll be rewarded with some serious improvements to how you look and feel

VISUALISE SUCCESS

The more you believe in your ability to complete a successful transformation, the more likely it is to happen. Several sports science studies have also shown that visualisation techniques can have a positive impact on performance.

MAKE IT WORK

At the start of each session, take a moment to remind yourself why you started the plan. Then think about how you'll look and feel when you achieve your desired result. You can use a similar process during a session when it becomes physically and mentally challenging. Struggling with that last rep? Mentally fast-forward and think about the satisfaction you'll get from a successful outcome and how you gave it 100% to get there.

APPLY TENSION

Learning to properly contract (apply tension to) a target muscle will have a huge impact on your capacity to burn fat and build muscle. Poor execution will lead to a poor result.

MAKE IT WORK

Whenever you complete a rep, make sure you think about the muscle you're trying to work and that you lift at a controlled pace rather than swinging the weight around and using momentum to move the load. You may find this means you need to lift a lighter weight. That's fine. Your body doesn't know how heavy the dumbbell is. All that counts is how you lift and how you stimulate the muscle fibres.

CALORIES COUNT

What you eat during the course of your plan has a massive impact on your overall result. To lose body fat you'll need to go into a calorie deficit and when that happens, what you eat matters more than ever.

MAKE IT WORK

If your calorie intake is limited then we advise that you aim to take in as many nutrients as possible. Eating nutrient-dense foods such as vegetables will support your overall health and immune system, which can be tested when you're training hard. Taking on good-quality protein will help you to repair and build muscle tissue. Those foods are also likely to help you feel satisfied even if you're eating less than usual.

TIMING MATTERS

Nutrient timing is a much-debated subject. In everyday life, it probably doesn't matter that much. But when you're doing a time-limited body transformation, it offers a potential incremental gain that's worth considering.

MAKE IT WORK

We recommend that you make sure you eat at least 30g of good-quality protein within an hour of finishing your workouts. That will help to repair the damage done to muscle fibres during the session. You can also eat more carbs after a training session to replenish your energy stores and help shuttle protein to your muscle cells.

Jon battled through illness and injury to end his plan with a cover shoot

HANG IN THERE

One of the biggest elements of a transformation is simply lasting the distance. At the start, or when you're tired or hungry, the finish line can seem an intimidatingly long way off. But take the plan day by day and you will get there.

MAKE IT WORK

The best news I can give you, having done the plan, is that it gets easier. The second half of your transformation challenge is easier than the first because you're fitter and your body has adapted to a new way of eating and using fat for fuel. Better still, the final block is the easiest of the four because the end is in sight and your new-found fitness will power you through. So if you're struggling, just remember that it gets easier. Trust me – the final week feels like a parade.

FOLLOW A PLAN

Without a plan you'll find that your training is aimless. You'll end up doing the same thing over and over again, you won't make progress and you'll lose motivation. It's vital that you follow a progressive plan that will help you make the most of your training time.

MAKE IT WORK

You've already made a smart choice in picking up the New Body Plan which, in just eight weeks, will transform how you look and feel forever. I've worried about the details so you don't have to. Simply follow the training plan to the letter and use the healthy eating advice, and you can look forward to being the proud owner of a brand new body.

50 WAYS TO UPGRADE YOUR BODY TRANSFORMATION

Get an amazing result with this tried and tested advice

EASY WINS

01 DON'T BE A MIRROR MAN

You're trying to change your body shape so it's only natural that you'll want to keep an eye on how you're doing. The problem is that it's hard to be objective when you're assessing your own physique. It's also almost impossible to see a difference from one day to the next, so even if you are making incremental improvements you'll feel like you're going nowhere and that's likely to dent your motivation. Admittedly, it's difficult to resist the temptation to look in the mirror all the time – but don't let what you see affect your mood. Instead, we advise you to...

02 TAKE WEEKLY PROGRESS SHOTS

You will notice a difference from week to week so either take a mirror selfie or get someone to take a picture of you once a week. Try to keep the conditions the same as much as possible, such as the time of day and the lighting, but don't obsess over those things. You will also find that your progress isn't consistent – some weeks you'll see a bigger change than others – but we guarantee that if you follow the plan, your before and after images will show a dramatic difference.

03 SCALE BACK

The scales are of limited use during your body transformation. One of the reasons is that if you weigh yourself on two different days, you could have lost fat but be carrying a bit more water, so the number on your scale could go up even if you've made genuine progress. You'll also add muscle during your eight-week transformation, which will affect how much you weigh.

04 A CRISP WON'T KILL YOU

If you change the way you eat, you can expect to experience cravings for the foods that you eliminate from your diet. If you usually eat a bag of crisps with lunch or have a bowl of ice cream every evening, your body becomes used to getting those foods and it'll take a bit of time to adjust. So don't be hard on yourself if you really miss them at the beginning of the plan. Tell yourself that you can have those treats in eight weeks' time – by which point you probably won't want them as much anyway. In fact, it's likely that after a couple of weeks the cravings will disappear. But if you do succumb to temptation it's important that you don't beat yourself up about it. Just move on and renew your focus on the plan.

05 GET AN ENERGY BURST

If you go from not training regularly and eating whatever you want to training several times a week and being careful with what you eat then, initially, you may feel a bit tired. The great news is that if you persist with the plan then your body will adjust and you'll soon feel fitter, healthier and more energised.

06 GO PUBLIC

There are a couple of reasons why you should do this. One of them is that by telling people you're doing a transformation you make yourself accountable. If you don't tell anyone, no-one will know when you give up after a couple of weeks. But if you tell lots of people then you'll be encouraged to persevere. You can also use your friends as a support group. Tell them that you need their help and they'll be less likely to push that packet of pork scratchings your way when you meet them in the pub. Or, even better...

07 DO THE CHALLENGE WITH A FRIEND

Whatever your fitness aim – whether it's doing a transformation challenge or training for a marathon – it's easier to achieve your goal when you do it with a friend. You can encourage and support each other during tough sessions, and you'll also find you don't want to let each other down, which means you'll be less likely to duck out of sets and reps or skip entire sessions.

08 SOCIALISE SMARTER

How easily your social life fits into your transformation challenge depends on how you're used to living your life. If you don't drink and your friends are more likely to be lifting a barbell than propping up a bar, then you may not encounter any obstacles. If, however, your social life involves sinking a few pints and the only veg you get is the salad on your post-pub kebab, you could be in for a tougher ride. Just try to get your friends onside and let them know how they can help. It's important that you don't become a hermit for eight weeks. Seeing friends is a vital part of good mental heath and it will provide a welcome distraction so that the transformation doesn't become all-consuming.

09 TALK TO YOUR PARTNER

This can be tough because your transformation may force your partner to think about how they feel about their own body and they may find that challenging. Body shape is an emotive subject and that's always something you should be aware of and sensitive about. There's also something inevitably selfish about a transformation challenge because your food choices will change, for example, which means you may not be able to eat the same meals as your partner. You'll also have to make time for your workouts. All you can do is be honest with your other half about what you're doing and why you're doing it and ask for their support.

10 THINK IN BLOCKS

One of the keys to a successful transformation is to track but not over-analyse your progress. As we said in point number one, daily scrutiny isn't helpful – it's more useful to split the eight-week period into manageable chunks. You're likely to see a noticeable difference from one week to the next, so treat each week or block as a mini goal. The world is set up to operate in week-long periods so it makes sense to fall into that structure. You can also get into useful routines, such as doing a shop for all the food you need for the week ahead.

11 BE HONEST

Doing a body transformation can be intense from both a physical and an emotional perspective. If you want to get the best result you can then it makes sense to be honest with yourself. If you go too easy and tell yourself that you're training hard so you can still have your Friday night beer and curry blow-out, you won't maximise your potential. Equally, being unnecessarily hard on yourself won't help either. If you're eating well, training hard and recovering sensibly then you're doing everything you can.

12 GOOD DAYS WILL COME

You can guarantee that some days will be amazing and you'll feel like you're going to smash it. On others you'll question why you're bothering to make the effort or whether your improvements are rapid enough. If you anticipate that this will happen, it will be less of a shock when you do experience highs and lows throughout the plan. Our advice is to spend ten minutes at the end of each week assessing how you felt during the past seven days. If you didn't feel as good as you wanted to, try to identify why that might have been the case and think of three things (big or small) that you can do to make progress next week.

13 ASK YOURSELF A QUESTION

Even if you are training with a friend, you still need to ask yourself this question before you start: "How much do I want this?" Quite simply, the stronger your starting motivation, the more likely it is that you'll get the result you want. After all, you are the master of your own destiny when it comes to a body transformation. You have to turn up, you have to lift the weights and you have to be in charge of what you eat. The more responsibility you take, the better the result you'll get.

NUTRITION ESSENTIALS

14 PROTEIN FIRST

The aim of your body transformation is to simultaneously lose fat and add muscle, and the best way of doing that is to prioritise high-quality protein intake from meat, fish and eggs. From there you should add healthy fats

(monounsaturated, polyunsaturated and saturated) and fill in the rest with carbohydrates. You'll find a complete guide to how to eat in the nutrition section, which starts on p136.

15 DON'T CHASE PERFECTION

The better your diet, the better your result will be. If you can eat well all of the time, great. But if you sense that's not realistic for you to stick to, it's perfectly OK to use our 90% Nutrition approach (see p144), where you eat well 90% of the time and take a more relaxed attitude for the remaining meals.

16 LIMIT BOOZE

Booze contains plenty of calories but few useful nutrients from a body transformation perspective, so if you don't limit your alcohol intake during the eight-week challenge then you'll struggle to lose fat and add muscle. If you really want to drink, our advice is to stick to clear spirits or red wine instead of white wine or lager.

17 EAT CARBS AROUND TRAINING

For non-athletes, nutrient timing probably isn't that important. But because your time and calorie intake are limited during the New Body Plan, it does become a significant factor. We recommend that you have a small amount of carbs a couple of hours before training so that you have enough energy to nail the session. Then have a portion of carbs (to complement your protein) in your post-workout meal. Find our Perfect Portion guide to meal building on p152.

18 MAX OUT ON VEG

Veg contains lots of nutrients that will help to support your general health and immune system, which is crucial during a time when you're asking a lot of your body. They also contain fibre and water, which will help you to feel satisfied and stay feeling full after your meal.

19 DRINK HEAVILY

Water, that is. Dehydration can easily be confused with hunger, so if you're not drinking enough water that could lead to eating more than you need to. Water is also essential for all manner of physiological processes, so it will help you stay healthy throughout your transformation challenge.

TRAIN SMARTER

20 LEAVE YOUR PHONE IN YOUR LOCKER

Your phone will be a distraction and anything that diverts attention from your training session will reduce the effectiveness of that workout. If you need it for a soundtrack, put it on Airplane mode or turn off notifications..

21 STAY FOCUSED

When you're in the gym the only thing you should be thinking about during a set is how to execute each rep

perfectly. When you're resting between sets you should use visualisation techniques to think about how to execute the set you're about to perform. That's it. Nothing else.

22 THINK OF YOURSELF AS AN ELITE ATHLETE

For these eight weeks we want you to imagine that you're a fighter preparing for a world title bout. If you have that mindset you're not going to slack off – and so you're more likely to get the results you want.

23 DO A THOROUGH WARM-UP

Sure, warm-ups are a bit dull, but they are important. They give you ten minutes to get your mind focused on what you're about to do. They also raise your heart rate, get blood flowing to your target muscles and ensure that the synovial fluid in your joints is working to prevent injury. For each exercise, do at least two light sets of the move before you get to your first "work" set.

24 PICK A TIME THAT SUITS YOU

The best time to train is the time you can stick to. You know what your schedule is going to be like and when you'll find time to train. Once you've identified that, write the sessions into your diary and treat them with the same significance as an important meeting.

25 USE (CONTROLLED) ANGER

A little bit of controlled aggression can have a positive impact on how you perform a rep, a set and a session. It will allow you to squeeze the final 5% out of your muscles. How you make yourself angry is up to you, but do yourself and your fellow gym-goers a favour and keep it controlled. No-one likes an aggro gym tosser.

26 DON'T BE AFRAID TO GRUNT

If you need to make a bit of a grunt (or, heck, a squeal) when you lift to get the most out of your muscles, go for it. In fact, if you don't have to make a bit of noise at the end of your last couple of reps of a set then you may not be working hard enough. Show-off grunting, on the other hand, isn't acceptable.

27 IGNORE YOUR BRAIN

Your brain is a wonderful but sometimes unhelpful thing. It will tell you to stop. It will tell you that you can't go on. Whatever you do, don't listen to it. Turn the volume down on that negative inner voice by repeating positive phrases such as "I can do this" under your breath when the going gets tough.

28 TAKE THE STAIRS

There are a lot of factors that influence fat loss but one of the central elements is using up more calories than you take in. You'll get most of the way there by increasing your gym workouts and being smarter with your food

Thinking of yourself
as an elite athlete
will help you get
high-level results

choices. But you'll also help yourself by using the remaining hours of the day to be a little bit more active. Over the course of eight weeks, doing a few simple things like taking the stairs instead of the lift can add up to have a surprisingly big impact on your physique.

29 ADD IN EXTRA LISS
Resistance training and high-intensity training, like the sessions detailed in this plan, put a fair amount of stress on your body. You can only do so much at the top end of your work capacity, so one simple way of increasing your activity is to add in some low-intensity steady state (LISS) work, such as going for a walk or a gentle cycle. It will burn extra calories, have a positive impact on your mental well-being and it may even help you prepare for your next session because staying mobile and getting blood and nutrients flowing into your muscles can accelerate recovery.

EAT SMARTER

30 DON'T SWEAT THE SLIP-UPS
During the course of eight weeks you'll consume about 112,000 calories. One glass of wine is about 140

calories. A doughnut is about 280 calories. So, in the grand scheme of things, a slip-up is going to make no difference to your overall progress. In fact, you'll probably do more harm by stressing about it or letting it sap your motivation. Of course, drinking alcohol or eating refined sugar regularly will derail your progress, but it's important to maintain a sense of perspective.

31 TAKE YOUR TIME
We live in a world where we do everything in a hurry but when it comes to how you eat, it pays to slow down. There are a couple of reasons for this. If you chew your food properly you'll digest it more effectively and assimilate more of the nutrients – which is particularly important when every calorie counts. You'll also be more receptive to your body telling you when you feel full, so you'll feel more satisfied at the end of a meal and you'll find it easier to resist the urge to overeat.

32 EAT AT A TABLE
Eating at a table, as opposed to in front of the television, will help you stay in control of what you eat. A recent analysis of studies looking into how people eat and their total food intake found that people eat more when they are distracted. The results, published in the *American*

Journal Of Clinical Nutrition, also revealed that "attentive eating" – where you focus on your food rather than on a screen – can help you control how much you eat.

33 DON'T RUSH BACK FOR A SECOND HELPING

How you eat, as well as how much, will have an influence on how full you feel. If you wolf down a plate of food, the chances are you'll still feel hungry when you finish. This is because your body hasn't had a chance to register what it has just eaten. So you go back for a second helping, thinking that you need the extra food. If you take your time, your satiety hormones will be able to work properly so you may not feel that you need a second helping. If you do feel hungry when you finish a meal, wait for ten minutes or so before deciding whether or not you want more. The chances are that your first portion will be enough.

34 CLEAN OUT YOUR CUPBOARDS

We all have a finite amount of willpower, so there's no point in wasting it. Let's say that you're used to cracking open an ice-cold bottle of beer when you get in at 7pm after a long and stressful day at work. If you start the plan and decide not to drink alcohol but you leave your nice cold bottles of beer lined up in the fridge, every time you open it you'll get a reminder of the thing you've decided not to have. You'll need to use up a tiny bit of willpower to resist the urge to reach for the bottle opener. But if you ensure there's none in the fridge before you start the plan, they'll be out of sight and, hopefully, out of mind. Use the same tactic for any other things you think you might be tempted by but are trying to limit during your transformation challenge.

35 NEVER SAY NEVER

When you say that you'll never do something, such as "I won't have any ice cream during my body transformation" then you put a lot of pressure on yourself. Instead, try telling yourself that you can have it tomorrow. When tomorrow comes, the chances are you either won't feel like it or you'll be in a stronger position from a willpower point of view. And if you still feel like it, tell yourself you'll have it tomorrow...

36 PREPARE TO SUCCEED

If you want to stand any chance of eating well then, as a minimum, we recommend that you make your breakfast and lunch the night before so they're ready for you to take out of the fridge in the morning. If you don't have a fridge at work, buy a small cool bag. And aim to bulk-buy your food each week. It'll save time and money.

PERFORM THE PERFECT REP

37 SQUEEZE THE TARGET MUSCLE

You may not end up looking like a bodybuilder but you can

To get the most out of every rep, make sure you squeeze the target muscle

borrow some of the big guys' techniques. At the top of each rep, squeeze the target muscle so that you feel it properly contract. The better the contraction, the better the outcome.

38 SQUEEZE THE AGONIST MUSCLE

The agonist muscle is the one on the opposite side to the target muscle. So, if you're training your biceps (the front of your upper arms), the agonist is the triceps (the back of your upper arms). Before you start each rep, squeeze the agonist muscle to ensure that you use a full range of motion and also send the right signals from brain to muscle to maximise muscle fibre recruitment.

39 MAKE EVERY REP LOOK THE SAME

You should be in control of the weight and each rep should look the same and take roughly the same time. The exception is the final couple of reps of each set, which you may have to fight for.

40 DON'T USE MOMENTUM

If you swing the weights around you aren't properly applying tension to the target muscle. And it's the

purposefully planting your feet, taking three deep breaths and visualising the first rep before you get the weights in place. You'll find that this will have positively impact your session.

44 CONTROL THE ECCENTRIC
The eccentric (lowering) phase of a lift is important because it's an opportunity to expose your muscle to stress in its strongest part of the lift. Take the bench press, for example. If you drop the bar to your chest, rather than controlling the lowering phase of the lift, you're missing out on a huge proportion of the exercise's potential benefit.

45 KEEP TENSION ON THE MUSCLE
Rather than jolting your joints and locking out on every rep, aim to maintain tension in the muscle by keeping a softness in your joints, particularly in machine and isolation moves. For heavy compound lifts, such as deadlifts, squats and bench presses it is safer to lock out each rep.

46 MAKE THE FIRST REP COUNT
You will always be comparatively fresh at the start of each set, so it's easy to switch off for the first couple of reps. Remember, they way you perform the first rep will determine the quality of your set.

47 SET UP TO BE STABLE
Before you lift, always brace your core by taking a breath and contracting your abs. It also makes sense to recruit your glutes to give your entire body more stability and make it more able to perform the lift.

48 GET YOUR BREATHING SORTED
Breathing properly will ensure that you are strong and stable in the key parts of a rep. Take a breath before you do a rep and exhale as you complete the rep, then take another breath and repeat the cycle.

49 SQUEEZE THE BAR
Squeezing the weight before you lift will send a signal to your brain to recruit muscle fibres and help you move the load. It will also help to get your mind focused so you can put maximum effort into the exercise.

MOTIVATION

50 ENJOY THE PROCESS
If you want it enough and you follow the plan, then in a short period of time you'll make a dramatic difference to how you look and feel. You'll feel healthier, happier and more energised. Sure, some sessions may be a bit of a battle, but take heart from the fact that every single rep of every single set will have a positive effect on your mind and your body, and every single day will take you closer to your goal.

application of tension, rather than the number on the weight, that really matters. Using momentum might help to grow your ego but it won't do much for your muscles.

41 THINK ABOUT THE MUSCLE
This is another old-school bodybuilder technique. You've probably heard of the mind-muscle connection, and it's real – studies have shown that thinking about the muscle you're trying to target will have a positive impact on the effectiveness of your session.

42 USE MENTAL CUES
Your overall goal should be to perform every rep as well as you can. One way of helping yourself get focused before the start of a set is to use a verbal or physical cue to tell your brain, "right, time to go to work". You could say the word "strong" to yourself. Or you could quickly tense your muscles. See what works for you.

43 CREATE A PRE-SET ROUTINE
To take the above idea a step further, you could create a pre-set routine. This could involve something along the lines of

SLEEP SOUNDER TONIGHT!

Along with training and nutrition, recovery is the third pillar of a successful body transformation. If you want to be ready for your next session, the most important thing you can do is make sure that you're getting a good night's sleep

There's supposed to be something very impressive about getting by with very little sleep. We hear highly successful people who get by with only four or five hours a night described as "superhuman". But there is nothing big or clever about surviving on minimal sleep. For people who are not natural "short-sleepers" (thought to be just 2% of the population), poor and disturbed sleep is a serious problem. Indeed, a recent UK poll found that only 50% of us are happy with the amount of sleep we get.

Poor sleep has serious consequences for your physical health – it's associated with increased risk of obesity and heart disease – and your mental health. It increases the risk of depression and mood disorders, and impairs decision-making, concentration, communication and language skills, among many other problems. But we have the solutions, so read on to learn how to sleep better – starting tonight!

The quality of your rest and recovery will have a huge impact on the outcome of your transformation challenge

Why is sleep so important? The truth is we still don't have a fully comprehensive answer, but new research is constantly shining the light on some possible explanations. For instance, during the day metabolic "debris" accumulates between the connections in the brain and impairs the ability of nerve cells to communicate. When you sleep the gaps between brain cells open up and spinal fluid flows in, flushing out this junk. If you don't get enough good-quality sleep this process is limited. A recent experiment that improved sleep among subjects was also successful at reducing depression, anxiety and paranoid thoughts. Here are seven ways you can start sleeping better.

1 KEEP COOL

A reduction in body temperature is a physiological indicator that it's nearly time for sleep. So if your room or bed is very hot, it makes it far harder to fall asleep and then stay asleep. Make sure you have the right tog duvet for the season and, at times when the nights are hotter, use a quiet fan if you need it. Taking a warm bath an hour before bed can also promote the onset of sleep because your body starts cooling down once you step out of the bath.

2 GET SOME SUN

Exposure to bright, natural light anchors your daily sleep/wake cycle in to a healthy rhythm. Try to get out and spend at least 30 minutes in daylight in the morning or take a half-hour walk after lunch.

3 HACK YOUR BODY CLOCK

You may have heard of the circadian rhythm, which is the scientific name for your 24-hour body clock, but what about the ultradian rhythm? This is a 90-minute cycle of processes in the body that repeats throughout the day, and tracking yours can help you identify the best time for you to go to bed.

The ultradian rhythm is remarkably consistent and you can track it by timing your yawns. At the peak of the wave you're at your most alert and it's the perfect time to tackle your to-do list, but 45 minutes later you're at the trough of the wave and most likely to yawn. So, if you yawn around 8.30pm

but it's too early to go to bed, you know you're likely to be most sleepy again at 10pm and then 11.30pm. Once you realise that you can then make sure you're in bed by 9.50pm or 11.20pm to get to sleep as quickly as possible.

4 PUT DOWN YOUR PHONE

Smartphones, tablets and computer screens emit blue light, which is the same wavelength as dawn light and is therefore interpreted by your brain as a sign that it's take time wake up, be alert and get active. To avoid this disrupting your sleep, try to avoid using your devices for at least an hour before bed – or at the very least turn on your devices' night-time setting so they shift from blue light to red light.

5 GET BLACKOUT CURTAINS

Make sure the bedroom is as dark and quiet as possible and use an eye mask, blackout curtains and ear plugs if you live in or near a noisy environment. Remember that every bit of light or sound pollution can affect your ability to fall asleep and sleep soundly.

6 CUT BACK ON BOOZE

Although alcohol promotes feelings of tiredness and can help you fall asleep, it disturbs your sleep quality by preventing your brain from entering the deeper, restorative phases of sleep. Try not to drink too much booze before going to bed, and cut back on all drinks in general: small-hours trips to the loo are very detrimental to a good night's sleep.

7 TRY TO RELAX!

There is no magic number to how much sleep you need. The right amount is enough for you not to feel excessively sleepy during the day. That might be seven hours or nine; we all have different sleep needs. Work out how much you think you need, then focus on getting that amount every night.

QUICK TIP

Good-quality sleep is essential to the health of your brain and body. The link between poor sleep and mood problems, weight gain, diabetes, severe depression and mental illness is clear. Put in the effort to improve your night-time routine and you should improve your physical health, energy, mood and well-being – not just this week or this month, but for years to come!

HOW TO KEEP A WORKOUT JOURNAL

Recording what you do every time you train is an essential component of transformation success. Here's what you need to know

Keeping a workout journal is one of the easiest but most effective things you can do to ensure that you stick to the plan and make good progress. Quite simply, all you need to do is record what you do in the gym. This will help you stick to the plan because you'll feel more connected to what you're doing if there is a tangible record of your efforts. It also helps to form part of your training ritual and it will help you get into the habit of executing your sessions as outlined in this plan. If you have a written record of what you have lifted you can use it to make sensible incremental increases in the weight you lift next time you attempt that exercise. Our advice is to get a notebook, take it on to the gym floor and fill it out between sets. If you've never done this before, ensure that you fill out the basic workout details as an absolute minimum and, if you can, try to include other items of information as outlined opposite.

WORKOUT DATA

You should record the number of sets and reps you perform for each exercise. Also note down the tempo of the lift (see p43 for details) as well as the rest you take between sets and exercises. The other important item of information is the weight you lift for each set. Having this information is the most basic way of assessing your progress. In this plan you do the same exercises in both weeks of a block, so try to lift more in the second week of each block than you did in the first.

NUTRITION INFO

It is useful to make a note of what you eat before, during and after your sessions so that you can assess how your nutrition intake is affecting your performance. Write down what you had for your pre-workout meal and when you had it, as well as any pre-workout supplements that you've consumed. If you take on anything during a workout, even if it is just water, note that down too. The final element to record is what you eat for your post-workout meal.

EXTRA ANALYSIS

If you are new to training you may find that recording tons of information every time you train is overwhelming. If that's the case, stick to the basics. But if you can deal with it, more information will help you analyse your performance. Write down the time of the workout and how much sleep you got the night before, and rate your quality of sleep out of ten. After each session, note what went well, what could be improved and anything that you'll try to do differently next time to boost your performance.

Keeping a workout journal will provide motivation and help you stick to the plan

In Block 1 – the first fortnight of your New Body Plan – the goal is for you to build solid strength using five sets of eight to ten reps, while also starting the process of adding lean muscle mass and burning body fat.

Building up your strength levels first is important because it will change your body for the better, as well as allowing you to lift heavier in the next blocks to maximise how much muscle you build.

Turn the page to discover how to follow this first part of the plan to the letter and start making positive changes to your body straight away.

GET STRONG IN BLOCK 1

Here's the theory behind the first two-week block of the plan
and all you need to know to get off to the best-possible start

GOAL

SPLIT

STRUCTURE

PROGRESSION

In this first fortnight of the plan your goal is simple: to create solid foundations from which you can build a bigger and leaner body. To this end, the first block of this eight-week programme has been designed to increase your strength levels, building stronger and more powerful muscles. This will start to re-shape your body by chipping away at body fat stores and creating the right stimulus for new lean muscle mass to be built. Not only this, but building these strong foundations first will also enable you to work harder and smarter in the subsequent blocks to burn fat faster while also adding lean muscle mass quickly.

The workout splits in this initial block are very easy to understand – they're simply split into upper-body sessions and lower-body sessions. This approach allows you to work all your major upper- or lower-body muscles hard, then give them time to recover before you train them again. You'll target your torso and arms twice a week, and your legs and abs twice a week too. A smart way to follow the plan this week, and every week, is to train on a Monday, Wednesday, Friday and then Saturday or Sunday to give your body as much time as possible to recover between sessions.

Every workout in this two-week block is made up of six different exercises, which you'll perform as straight sets. This means you do all the sets and reps of exercise 1, sticking to the tempo and rest periods detailed, and then move on to exercise 2, and do all the sets and reps, and so on until you finish all the reps of the final set of exercise 6. This approach is both easy to follow and the smartest lifting strategy to use when working towards increasing strength levels.

The second week of the fortnight is very similar to the first week – you perform two upper-body and two lower-body sessions, each comprising the same exercises in the same order. There is, however, one major difference to help you get stronger faster. In week 2 you'll do fewer reps per set than in the first week, but you'll do an extra full set. This strategy is designed to help you lift heavier weights for each exercise in the second week. Even if you only increase the weights a small amount, it's important to try to lift heavier because that's what makes your muscles grow stronger.

TEMPO

In every workout table in this plan you'll see a column marked "Tempo", in between the "Reps" and "Rest" columns. In this column, each exercise has a four-digit number. Tempo is the speed at which you perform one rep of an exercise, and the four-digit number is the time in seconds you take to lift and lower the weight, and pause at the top and bottom. For example, a 2010 tempo for the bench press means you lower the bar to your chest in two seconds, with no pause at the bottom, then lift the bar in one second, with no pause at the top. An "X" tempo means you perform each rep explosively, but still with perfect form.

WEEK 1 SESSION 1

UPPER BODY	SETS	REPS	TEMPO	REST
1 Dumbbell bench press	3	10	2010	60sec
2 Lat pull-down	3	10	2011	60sec
3 Dumbbell shoulder press	3	10	2010	60sec
4 Dumbbell biceps curl	3	10	2011	60sec
5 Cable triceps press-down	3	10	2011	60sec
6 Press-up	3	10	2010	60sec

1 DUMBBELL BENCH PRESS

Sets 3 Reps 10 Tempo 2010 Rest 60sec

TARGETS Chest, triceps, front shoulders

TOP TIP
Breathe in as you lower the weights, then breathe out powerfully as you press them back up.

FORM GUIDE

- Lie on a bench, holding a dumbbell in each hand at chest height. Plant your feet on the floor directly underneath your knees.
- Brace your core and back muscles, and press your feet into the ground.
- Keeping your whole body tight and your chest up, press the weights directly up until your arms are straight and the weights touch over the middle of your chest.
- Slowly lower the weights back to the start position under complete control.
- Don't "bounce" the weights at the bottom of a rep to help initiate the next one. Instead keep each rep smooth and controlled.

2 LAT PULL-DOWN

Sets 3 Reps 10 Tempo 2011 Rest 60sec

TARGETS Lats, biceps

TOP TIP
When seated, your arms should be fully straight when holding the bar ahead of starting each rep.

FORM GUIDE

- Take a shoulder-width overhand grip on the bar and sit on the seat with your knees under the padded bar and your feet flat on the floor.
- Keeping your chest up, core braced and feet on the floor, pull the bar down towards your chin, leading with your elbows.
- Pause at the bottom of the rep and squeeze your lats as hard as you can, then return the bar back to the top position slowly and under control.

3 DUMBBELL SHOULDER PRESS

Sets **3** Reps **10** Tempo **2010** Rest **60sec**

TARGETS Shoulders, triceps

TOP TIP
Pushing your feet down into the floor and tensing your abs will help you power through those final reps.

FORM GUIDE

- Stand tall with your chest up and core braced, holding a dumbbell in each hand at shoulder-height with your palms facing away from you.
- Keeping your chest up and abs engaged, press the weights directly overhead until your arms are straight and the weights touch above your head.
- Slowly lower the weights back to the start position under complete control and keep each rep smooth without any bouncing.

4 DUMBBELL BICEPS CURL

Sets **3** Reps **10** Tempo **2011** Rest **60sec**

TARGETS Biceps

TOP TIP
Squeezing your biceps at the top then flexing your triceps at the bottom ensures you lift through a full range of motion.

FORM GUIDE

- Stand tall with your chest up and core braced, holding a dumbbell in each hand with your arms straight and your elbows by your sides with your palms facing away from you.
- Keeping your chest up and your elbows tight to your sides, curl the weights up towards shoulder height.
- Squeeze your biceps hard at the top of the rep, then slowly lower the weights back to the start under complete control.
- Straighten your arms fully at the bottom, flexing your triceps hard before you start the next rep.

5 CABLE TRICEPS PRESS-DOWN

Sets **3** Reps **10** Tempo **2011** Rest **60sec**

TARGETS Triceps, lower chest

TOP TIP
Holding the bottom position for a second increases the tension on your triceps to make them grow faster.

FORM GUIDE

- Stand tall in front of a cable machine with your chest up and core engaged, using both hands to hold a double rope handle attached to the high pulley.
- Keeping your chest up and your elbows tight to your sides, press your hands down until your arms are fully straight.
- Hold this bottom position and flex your triceps to keep the tension on them.
- Slowly return to the start position, without letting your elbows move away from your sides at any point.
- When you return to the top position, squeeze your biceps.

6 PRESS-UP

Sets **3** Reps **10** Tempo **2010** Rest **60sec**

TARGETS Chest, triceps, front shoulders

TOP TIP
Imagine you're pushing the floor away from you at the bottom of each press-up to powerfully return to the top.

FORM GUIDE

- Get on all fours with your legs and arms straight, your hands under your shoulders and your body in a straight line from head to heels.
- Raise your hips and brace your core to keep your entire body stable.
- Bend your elbows to lower your chest towards the floor, but don't let them flare out to the sides – they should stay tight to your sides.
- Go as low as you can, then press back up to straighten your arms and return to the start position.

WEEK 1 SESSION 2

LOWER BODY	SETS	REPS	TEMPO	REST
1 Dumbbell lunge	3	12	2010	60sec
2 Goblet squat	3	12	2010	60sec
3 Dumbbell step-up	3	12	1010	60sec
4 Bodyweight squat	3	25	2010	60sec
5 Crunch	3	12	1111	60sec
6 Plank jack	3	20	1010	60sec

1 DUMBBELL LUNGE

Sets 3 Reps 12 Tempo 2010 Rest 60sec

TARGETS Quads, glutes, hamstrings, core

TOP TIP
Make sure you take a big enough step forwards to start each rep to give yourself space to fully lunge down.

FORM GUIDE

- Stand tall with your chest up and your abs engaged, holding a dumbbell in each hand.
- Take a big step forwards with one foot, then lunge down until both knees are bent at right angles.
- Push off your front foot to return to the start and repeat, leading with your other leg.
- Continue, alternating your leading leg, until you have done 12 reps in total.

2 GOBLET SQUAT

Sets 3 Reps 12 Tempo 2010 Rest 60sec

TARGETS Quads, glutes, hamstrings, core

TOP TIP
If you use a dumbbell, hold it vertically in both hands. With a kettlebell, grasp each side of the handle.

FORM GUIDE

- Stand tall with your chest up and core engaged, holding a dumbbell or kettlebell at chest height with both hands, as you would hold a goblet.
- Keeping your chest up and back straight, initiate the move by bending your knees and pushing your hips backwards to squat down until your elbows brush the insides of your knees.
- Keep your weight on your heels and press down through them to straighten your legs and return to the start position.

3 DUMBBELL STEP-UP

Sets 3 Reps 12 Tempo 1010 Rest 60sec

TARGETS Quads, glutes, hamstrings, calves, core

FORM GUIDE

- Stand tall in front of a raised platform or bench, holding a dumbbell in each hand.
- Keeping your chest up and your core engaged, step up onto the raised surface with one foot, then the other.
- Step back down, leading with the foot that stepped up first. That's one rep.
- Alternate your leading foot with each rep, keeping your torso upright throughout the set.

TOP TIP
Squeeze your glutes at the start of each rep and when both feet are on the bench, so you keep these muscles switched on.

4 BODYWEIGHT SQUAT

Sets 3 Reps 25 Tempo 2010 Rest 60sec

TARGETS Quads, glutes, hamstrings, core

FORM GUIDE

- Stand tall with your chest up, abs engaged and arms straight by your sides.
- Bend your knees to squat down as low as you can, either keeping your arms by your sides or raising them up to shoulder height.
- Push through your heels to straighten your legs and return to the start position.

TOP TIP
In this high-rep set, keep each squat smooth and controlled, so you don't "bounce" out from the bottom position.

5 CRUNCH

Sets 3 Reps 12 Tempo 1111 Rest 60sec
TARGETS Upper abs

TOP TIP
Really try to hold the top position of each crunch for one second to increase the muscular tension on your abs.

FORM GUIDE

- Lie flat on your back with your knees bent and feet flat on the floor, and bend your arms so your fingers touch the sides of your head.
- Engage your abs, then raise your torso off the floor without tensing your neck.
- Keep the tension on your abs as you slowly lower your torso back to the floor.
- Make each rep harder by not allowing your upper back to touch the floor between reps.

6 PLANK JACK

Sets 3 Reps 20 Tempo 1010 Rest 60sec
TARGETS Core, lower abs

TOP TIP
As well as engaging your core, squeeze your glutes before you start the first rep to make your entire body stable.

FORM GUIDE

- Get into position, supporting yourself on your forearms with your elbows underneath your shoulders.
- Engage your abs, then raise your hips so that your body forms a straight line from head to heels.
- Imagine you're trying to draw your bellybutton in towards your spine to fire up all the muscles of your core, then hold this position.
- Without letting your hips sag, jump both feet out to the sides so your toes tap the floor, then jump your feet back in. Keep repeating this movement.
- Keep your head and neck relaxed and keep your breathing controlled – don't hold your breath.

WEEK 1 SESSION 3

UPPER BODY	SETS	REPS	TEMPO	REST
1 Incline dumbbell bench press	3	10	2010	60sec
2 Seated row	3	10	2011	60sec
3 Dumbbell lateral raise	3	10	2011	60sec
4 Dumbbell hammer curl	3	10	2011	60sec
5 Cable overhead triceps extension	3	10	2011	60sec
6 Press-up	3	10	2010	60sec

1 INCLINE DUMBBELL BENCH PRESS

Sets 3 Reps 10 Tempo 2010 Rest 60sec

TARGETS Upper chest, triceps, front shoulders

TOP TIP
The higher the incline of the bench, the more the move targets your upper chest and shoulders.

FORM GUIDE

- Lie on an incline bench, holding a dumbbell in each hand at chest height. Plant your feet on the floor directly underneath your knees.
- Brace your core and back muscles, and press your feet into the ground.
- Keeping your whole body tight and your chest up, press the weights directly up until your arms are straight and the weights touch over the middle of your chest.
- Slowly lower the weights back down to the start position under complete control.
- Don't "bounce" the weights at the bottom of a rep to help initiate the next one. Instead keep each rep smooth and controlled.

2 SEATED ROW

Sets 3 Reps 10 Tempo 2010 Rest 60sec

TARGETS Upper back, biceps

TOP TIP
During each rep keep your torso as stable and stationary as possible – only your arms should move with each row.

FORM GUIDE

- Position yourself on the machine with your feet against the foot rest, holding a double-grip cable attachment in both hands.
- Keeping your chest up, back straight and core braced, row your hands in towards your body, leading with your elbows.
- Once your hands are by your body, pause for a second and squeeze your back and biceps muscles hard, then reverse the move back to the start position.

3 DUMBBELL LATERAL RAISE

Sets 3 Reps 10 Tempo 2011 Rest 60sec

TARGETS Side shoulders

TOP TIP
Make your muscles do all the work and minimise momentum by using light weights and sticking to proper form.

FORM GUIDE

- Stand tall with your chest up, abs braced and feet hip-width apart, holding a light dumbbell in each hand by your sides with your palms facing one another.
- Keeping a slight bend in your elbows, raise the weights out to the sides, no higher than shoulder height.
- As the weights approach shoulder height, rotate your wrists slightly so that your little fingers are pointing straight up – this will contract your side delts harder.
- Pause and hold this top position for a second, then slowly lower the weights back to the start under complete control.

4 DUMBBELL HAMMER CURL

Sets 3 Reps 10 Tempo 2011 Rest 60sec

TARGETS Biceps, forearms

TOP TIP
Keep your elbows locked in position – if your form breaks down, use lighter weights or curl one arm at a time.

FORM GUIDE

- Stand tall with your chest up, core braced and shoulders back, holding a pair of dumbbells with your palms facing your sides.
- Keeping your elbows tight to your sides, curl the dumbbells up towards your shoulders.
- At the top position pause and squeeze your biceps hard, then slowly lower the weights back to the start under complete control.
- Fully straighten your arm and flex your triceps at the bottom of each rep to ensure your biceps muscles move through a full range of motion.

5 CABLE OVERHEAD TRICEPS EXTENSION

Sets **3** Reps **10** Tempo **2011** Rest **60**sec
TARGETS Triceps

FORM GUIDE

- Stand tall with your back to a cable machine with your chest up and core engaged, holding a double rope handle in both hands behind your head attached to low pulley.
- Lean forwards slightly from your hips, but keep your chest up and your back straight.
- Keeping your elbows locked in position either side of your head and pointing straight up, press your hands up and forwards to straighten your arms.
- When your arms are fully straight, pause and flex your triceps for one second. Slowly return your hands back to the start position, then squeeze your biceps hard before starting the next rep.

6 PRESS-UP

Sets **3** Reps **10** Tempo **2010** Rest **60**sec
TARGETS Chest, triceps, front shoulders

FORM GUIDE

- Get on all fours with your legs and arms straight, your hands under your shoulders and your body in a straight line from head to heels.
- Raise your hips and brace your core to keep your entire body stable.
- Bend your elbows to lower your chest towards the floor, but don't let them flare out to the sides – they should stay tight to your sides.
- Go as low as you can, then press back up to straighten your arms and return to the start position.

WEEK 1 SESSION 4

LOWER BODY	SETS	REPS	TEMPO	REST
1 Dumbbell lunge	3	12	2010	60sec
2 Goblet squat	3	12	2010	60sec
3 Leg extension	3	12	2011	60sec
4 Hamstring curl	3	12	2011	60sec
5 Bicycle	3	20	1111	60sec
6 Plank toe tap	3	20	1111	60sec

1 DUMBBELL LUNGE

Sets 3 Reps 12 Tempo 2010 Rest 60sec
TARGETS Quads, glutes, hamstrings, core

TOP TIP
Before the first rep and every subsequent rep, push your hips forwards, squeeze your glutes and brace your abs.

FORM GUIDE

- Stand tall with your chest up and your abs engaged, holding a dumbbell in each hand.
- Take a big step forwards with one foot, then lunge down until both knees are bent at right angles.
- Push off your front foot to return to the start and repeat, leading with your other leg.
- Continue, alternating your leading leg, until you have done 12 reps in total.

2 GOBLET SQUAT

Sets 3 Reps 12 Tempo 2010 Rest 60sec
TARGETS Quads, glutes, hamstrings, core

TOP TIP
When holding the weight in position, press your elbows tight to your sides to keep your back straight and torso stable.

FORM GUIDE

- Stand tall with your chest up and core engaged, holding a dumbbell or kettlebell at chest height with both hands, as you would hold a goblet.
- Keeping your chest up and back straight, initiate the move by bending your knees and pushing your hips backwards to squat down until your elbows brush the insides of your knees.
- Keep your weight on your heels and press down through them to straighten your legs and return to the start position.

3 LEG EXTENSION

Sets 3 Reps 12 Tempo 2011 Rest 60sec

TARGETS Quads

TOP TIP
Don't rush the reps or swing your feet up and down. Take your time and really think about squeezing your quads.

FORM GUIDE

- Prepare the machine, following the instructions to make the necessary adjustments so when you sit on it you're positioned correctly and safely.
- In the start position you should be sitting upright with your chest up and shins against the padded bar.
- Raise the bar by raising your feet until both legs are fully straight.
- Hold this top position for one second, keeping the maximum amount of tension on your quads, then slowly lower your feet back to the start position.

4 HAMSTRING CURL

Sets 3 Reps 12 Tempo 2011 Rest 60sec

TARGETS Hamstrings

TOP TIP
This move may feel uncomfortable if you're not used to hamstring training, so start light and focus on good form.

FORM GUIDE

- Prepare the machine, following the instructions to make the necessary adjustments so when you sit on it you're positioned correctly and safely.
- In the start position you should be sitting upright with your chest up and straight legs, with the padded bar against the back of your ankles, above your heel.
- Lower the bar by bending your knees and pulling your feet down underneath your body.
- Hold this bottom position for one second, keeping the maximum amount of tension on your hamstrings, then slowly raise your feet back to the start position.

5 BICYCLE

Sets 3 Reps 12 Tempo 1111 Rest 60sec

TARGETS Core, side abs

TOP TIP
A 1111 tempo means 1sec to raise your limbs, a 1sec hold at the top, 1sec to lower and a 1sec pause at the bottom.

FORM GUIDE

- Lie flat on your back with your fingers by your temples and legs straight.
- Raise your torso off the floor, engage your abs, and then lift your feet off the floor.
- Crunch up and rotate your torso to one side, bringing your opposite knee in to touch your elbow.
- Reverse the movement to return to the starting position – without your upper back or feet touching the floor – then repeat on the other side.
- When you've rotated to both sides and returned to the start, that's one reps. Continue, alternating sides.

6 PLANK TOE TAP

Sets 3 Reps 12 Tempo 1111 Rest 60sec

TARGETS Core, abs

TOP TIP
Use the 1111 tempo as a rhythm so each rep is smooth, and don't let the tension off your core until the set is over.

FORM GUIDE

- Get into a plank position, supporting yourself on your forearms with your elbows underneath your shoulders.
- Engage your abs, then raise your hips so that your body forms a straight line from head to heels. Keep that tension on your core and squeeze your glutes.
- Without letting your hips sag, lift and move one foot out as far as you can to the side.
- Tap your toe down on the floor then bring it back in and repeat with the other foot. That's one rep.

WEEK 2 **SESSION 1**

UPPER BODY	SETS	REPS	TEMPO	REST
1 Dumbbell bench press	4	8	2010	60sec
2 Lat pull-down	4	8	2011	60sec
3 Dumbbell shoulder press	4	8	2010	60sec
4 Dumbbell biceps curl	4	8	2011	60sec
5 Cable triceps press-down	4	8	2011	60sec
6 Press-up	4	10	2010	60sec

WEEK 2 **SESSION 2**

LOWER BODY	SETS	REPS	TEMPO	REST
1 Dumbbell lunge	4	10	2010	60sec
2 Goblet squat	4	10	2010	60sec
3 Dumbbell step–up	4	10	1010	60sec
4 Bodyweight squat	4	25	2010	60sec
5 Crunch	4	12	1111	60sec
6 Plank jack	4	20	1010	60sec

WEEK 2 **SESSION 3**

UPPER BODY	SETS	REPS	TEMPO	REST
1 Incline dumbbell bench press	4	8	2010	60sec
2 Seated row	4	8	2011	60sec
3 Dumbbell lateral raise	4	8	2011	60sec
4 Dumbbell hammer curl	4	8	2011	60sec
5 Cable overhead triceps extension	4	8	2011	60sec
6 Press-up	4	10	2010	60sec

WEEK 2 **SESSION 4**

LOWER BODY	SETS	REPS	TEMPO	REST
1 Dumbbell lunge	4	12	2010	60sec
2 Goblet squat	4	12	2010	60sec
3 Leg extension	4	12	2011	60sec
4 Hamstring curl	4	12	2011	60sec
5 Bicycle	4	20	1111	60sec
6 Plank toe tap	4	20	1111	60sec

Now that you've built a solid foundation of strength thanks to the workouts in the first block, it's time to take advantage of that new-found strength and start building as much lean, hard muscle mass as possible, while continuing to eat away at your body fat stores.

You'll add muscle fast by moving to a body part-specific training schedule and the inclusion of supersets – a tried-and-tested technique that adds lean size and strips away fat. Turn the page to learn more about the significant changes in this block of the plan, and how you can put it into action perfectly to continue your journey to building your best ever body.

GET BIG IN BLOCK 2

The core focus in this block is to add lean muscle mass as quickly and efficiently as possible, while still working to reduce body fat levels

GOAL

SPLIT

STRUCTURE

PROGRESSION

Having used the first block to build a baseline of strength, the goal in this second block is simple: to pack as much new lean muscle mass as possible onto your frame to accelerate your progress towards a bigger, stronger and leaner body. Adding lean muscle mass to your body, combined with continuing to burn fat, will make a big difference to your physique and how you look with your shirt off. To keep your positive body transformation changes coming, there are some significant changes to the workouts and their structure in this block, which we'll explain fully here.

One big change in this block from the previous one is the move from an upper-body and lower-body session split to one that specifies individual body parts. Your four weekly workout splits in this block will be chest and back; legs and abs; biceps and triceps; and shoulders and abs. It's this increased focus and dedicated training time on targeting specific muscle groups each session that will enable you to build new muscle tissue faster and continue your positive body composition changes.

As in block 1, every workout in this block contains six different exercises. However, now these six moves are paired into three supersets. Quite simply, a superset is two different moves done back to back with little or no rest between them. For instance, in the first workout of this block you'll do move 1A, which is ten reps of incline dumbbell bench press, rest for 30 seconds, then do move 1B, which is ten reps of the dumbbell prone row. After those reps you rest for 60 seconds, then go back to move 1A and so on, until you've done all the sets detailed. Then you move on and do the same for moves 2A and 2B, and 3A and 3B.

The supersets in this block are known as "antagonistic supersets" because the two moves work antagonistic (opposing) muscle groups. This is a highly effective approach for building muscle fast because one muscle group works while the other recovers. It also keeps your heart rate elevated for longer to burn more calories. In the first week you'll do four sets of the moves 1A and 1B, then three sets of moves 2A and 2B, and 3A and 3B. In the second week the set structure remains the same, but you will do more reps per set to give your body the additional stimulus to build more muscle and burn more fat.

WEEK 3 **SESSION 1**

CHEST AND BACK	SETS	REPS	TEMPO	REST
1A Incline dumbbell hammer press	4	10	2010	30sec
1B Dumbbell prone row	4	10	2011	60sec
2A Machine chest press	3	12	2010	30sec
2B Wide lat pull-down	3	12	2011	60sec
3A Cable flye	3	12	2011	30sec
3B Cable straight-arm pull-down	3	12	2011	60sec

1A INCLINE DUMBBELL HAMMER PRESS

Sets 4 Reps 10 Tempo 2010 Rest 30sec
TARGETS Chest, triceps, front shoulders

TOP TIP
Squeeze the handles of the dumbbells hard before the first rep of each set to fire up the target muscles.

FORM GUIDE

- Lie on an incline bench, holding a dumbbell in each hand at chest height with palms facing one another.
- Brace your core and back muscles, and press your feet into the ground.
- Keeping your whole body tight and your chest up, press the weights directly up until your arms are straight and the weights touch over the middle of your chest.
- Slowly lower the weights back to the start position under complete control.
- Don't "bounce" the weights at the bottom of a rep to help initiate the next one. Instead keep each rep smooth and controlled.

1B DUMBBELL PRONE ROW

Sets 4 Reps 10 Tempo 2011 Rest 60sec
TARGETS Back, biceps

TOP TIP
Set the bench at a high enough incline so that both your arms are fully straight at the start position of the move.

FORM GUIDE

- Lie chest-first on an incline bench, holding a dumbbell in each hand with straight arms and palms facing.
- Keeping your chest against the bench, row the weights up, leading with your elbows.
- At the top position pause and hold, squeezing your upper back hard, then slowly lower the weights back to the start.

2A MACHINE CHEST PRESS

Sets **3** Reps **12** Tempo **2010** Rest **30sec**

TARGETS Chest, triceps, front shoulders

FORM GUIDE

- Prepare the machine, following the instructions to make the necessary adjustments so when you sit on it you're positioned correctly and safely.
- In the start position you should be sitting upright with your chest up and holding the handles with a wider than shoulder-width overhand grip.
- Take a deep breath in, then breathe out forcefully and press the handles forwards to straighten your arms.
- Bend your elbows and slowly return to the start position.

TOP TIP
Don't jerk back and forth – keep each rep smooth to reduce the strain on your wrists, elbows and shoulders.

2B WIDE LAT PULL-DOWN

Sets **3** Reps **12** Tempo **2011** Rest **60sec**

TARGETS Back, biceps

FORM GUIDE

- Position yourself on the machine with a double shoulder-width overhand grip on the bar.
- Keeping your chest up, abs braced and back straight, pull the bar down to chin height, leading with your elbows.
- Hold the bottom position for a second, squeezing your lats hard, then reverse the movement back to the start.

TOP TIP
Your torso shouldn't move during a rep. If you have to rock back to pull the bar down, the weight is too heavy.

3A CABLE FLYE

Sets 3 Reps 12 Tempo 2011 Rest 30sec
TARGETS Chest

FORM GUIDE

- Stand tall with a split stance in the middle of a cable machine, holding a D-handle in each hand attached to the high pulley.
- Keeping your chest up, core braced and a slight bend in your elbows, bring your hands down in a smooth arc to meet in front of your chest.
- Hold this bottom position for one second, squeezing your chest muscles hard, then reverse the movement back to the start.

3B CABLE STRAIGHT-ARM PULL-DOWN

Sets 3 Reps 12 Tempo 2011 Rest 60sec
TARGETS Back

FORM GUIDE

- Stand tall in front of a cable machine, holding a straight-bar handle attached to the high pulley in both hands with an overhand grip and straight arms.
- Bend forwards slightly from the hips and, keeping your chest up, your abs braced and your arms straight, pull the bar down in a smooth arc so it hits your thighs.
- Hold this bottom position for one second, squeezing your lats hard, then reverse the movement back to the start.

WEEK 3 **SESSION 2**

LEGS AND ABS	SETS	REPS	TEMPO	REST
1A Front squat	4	10	2010	30sec
1B Romanian deadlift	4	10	2010	60sec
2A Leg extension	3	12	2011	30sec
2B Hamstring curl	3	12	2011	60sec
3A Hanging knee raise	3	12	1111	30sec
3B Hanging knee twist	3	12	1111	60sec

1A FRONT SQUAT

Sets 4 Reps 10 Tempo 2010 Rest 30sec
TARGETS Quads, hamstrings, glutes

TOP TIP
Pointing your toes out helps your knees push outwards to drive back to the top and prevent your knees rolling inwards.

FORM GUIDE

- Hold the bar across the front of your shoulders, either holding it in your hands with your elbows forward and upper arms parallel to the ground, or with your arms bent and crossed and your fingers resting on the opposite shoulder.
- Stand with your feet at least hip-width apart and your toes pointing slightly outwards to the sides.
- Keeping your elbows up, chest up and core engaged, squat down until your thighs are at least parallel to the floor.
- From this bottom position, drive through your heels, pushing your knees out to the sides, to stand back up to the start position.

1B ROMANIAN DEADLIFT

Sets 4 Reps 10 Tempo 2010 Rest 60sec
TARGETS Hamstrings, glutes

TOP TIP
Keep knee bend to a minimum – too much will "switch off" your hamstrings. If it's a problem, lighten the bar.

FORM GUIDE

- Stand tall with your feet shoulder-width apart, holding a barbell with an overhand grip just outside your thighs.
- With a slight bend in your knees, bend forwards from the hips and lower the bar down the front of your legs until you feel a good stretch in your hamstrings.
- Reverse the movement back to the start and push your hips forwards at the top.

2A LEG EXTENSION

Sets 3 Reps 12 Tempo 2011 Rest 30sec
TARGETS Quads

FORM GUIDE

- Prepare the machine, following the instructions to make the necessary adjustments so when you sit on it you're positioned correctly and safely.
- In the start position you should be sitting upright with your chest up and shins against the padded bar.
- Raise the bar by raising your feet until both legs are fully straight.
- Hold this top position for one second, keeping the maximum amount of tension on your quads, then slowly lower your feet back to the start position.

2B HAMSTRING CURL

Sets 3 Reps 12 Tempo 2011 Rest 60sec
TARGETS Hamstrings

FORM GUIDE

- Prepare the machine, following the instructions to make the necessary adjustments so when you sit on it you're positioned correctly and safely.
- In the start position you should be sitting upright with your chest up and straight legs, with the padded bar against the back of your ankles, above your heel.
- Lower the bar by bending your knees and pulling your feet down underneath your body.
- Hold this bottom position for one second, keeping the maximum amount of tension on your hamstrings, then slowly return your feet back to the start position.

3A HANGING KNEE RAISE

Sets 3 Reps 12 Tempo 1111 Rest 30sec
TARGETS Core, lower abs

TOP TIP
Don't take the tension off your core when you straighten your legs at the bottom of each rep. Keep those abs tight!

FORM GUIDE

- Position yourself in the machine or hang from a bar with a shoulder-width overhand grip and straight legs.
- Brace your core and glutes and with your feet together, draw your knees up towards your chest.
- Hold this position, then straighten your legs to return to the start position.

3B HANGING KNEE TWIST

Sets 3 Reps 12 Tempo 1111 Rest 60sec
TARGETS Core, side abs

TOP TIP
Don't hold your breath! Instead, breathe in as you raise your knees, and then out as you twist from side to side.

FORM GUIDE

- Position yourself in the machine or hang from a bar with a shoulder-width overhand grip and straight legs.
- Brace your core and glutes and with your feet together, draw your knees up towards your chest. Then twist your knees to one side, pause, then twist them across to the other side.
- Twist them back to the middle then straighten your legs to return to the start position. That's one rep.

WEEK 3 **SESSION 3**

BICEPS AND TRICEPS	SETS	REPS	TEMPO	REST
1A Incline close-grip bench press	4	10	2010	30sec
1B Underhand lat pull-down	4	10	2011	60sec
2A Standing EZ-bar biceps curl	3	12	2011	30sec
2B Lying EZ-bar triceps extension	3	12	2011	60sec
3A Cable hammer curl	3	12	2011	30sec
3B Cable triceps press-down	3	12	2011	60sec

1A INCLINE CLOSE-GRIP BENCH PRESS

Sets 4 Reps 10 Tempo 2010 Rest 30sec
TARGETS Triceps, chest, front shoulders

TOP TIP
If you're training alone, use a bench where you can rack and re-rack the bar safely or ask someone to spot you.

FORM GUIDE

- Lie on an incline bench with a shoulder-width overhand grip on the bar with straight arms.
- Brace your core and back muscles, and press your feet into the ground.
- Keeping your whole body tight and your chest up, lower the bar towards your chest under complete control.
- Lower the bar down until it touches your chest, then powerfully press it back up to the start position.
- Don't "bounce" the bar on your chest at the bottom of a rep to help initiate the next one. Instead keep each rep smooth and controlled.

1B UNDERHAND LAT PULL-DOWN

Sets 4 Reps 10 Tempo 2011 Rest 60sec
TARGETS Biceps, back

TOP TIP
Don't allow your head or torso to move during a rep – only your arms should move, otherwise the weight is too heavy.

FORM GUIDE

- Prepare the machine, following the instructions to make the necessary adjustments so when you sit on it you're positioned correctly and safely.
- In the start position you should be sitting with your knees secured, holding a straight bar with a shoulder-width underhand grip.
- Keeping your chest up and abs braced, pull the bar down to chin height, leading with your elbows.
- Hold the bottom position for a second, squeezing your biceps and back hard, then reverse the movement back to the start.

2A STANDING EZ-BAR BICEPS CURL

Sets **3** Reps **12** Tempo **2011** Rest **30sec**

TARGETS Biceps

TOP TIP
Try taking a narrower grip on the EZ-bar if that places less strain on your wrist, elbow and shoulder joints.

FORM GUIDE

- Stand tall with your chest up, abs braced and elbows by your sides, holding an EZ-bar using an underhand grip with your hands just outside your hips.
- Keeping your elbows tucked in to your sides, curl the bar up, stopping just before your forearms reach vertical.
- Pause in this top position for one second, squeezing your biceps hard.
- Slowly lower the bar back to the start position.

2B LYING EZ-BAR TRICEPS EXTENSION

Sets **3** Reps **12** Tempo **2011** Rest **60sec**

TARGETS Triceps

TOP TIP
You don't need to go heavy with this move. Start light and use good form to really "feel" it working your triceps.

FORM GUIDE

- Lie on a flat bench, holding an EZ-bar with a shoulder-width overhand grip and with straight arms.
- Brace your core and back muscles, and press your feet into the ground.
- Keeping your chest up and elbows pointing straight up to the ceiling, lower the bar towards the top of your head under complete control.
- Pause in this bottom position for one second, then press the bar back up to the top.
- Don't "bounce" the bar back up from the bottom position, which will place excess stress on your shoulder, elbow and wrist joints.

3A CABLE HAMMER CURL

Sets 3 Reps 12 Tempo 2011 Rest 30sec
TARGETS Biceps

TOP TIP
If your elbows move forwards it'll take tension off your biceps, so really press them into your sides.

FORM GUIDE

- Stand tall in front of a cable machine with your chest up and core engaged, using both hands to hold a double rope handle attached to the low pulley.
- Keeping your chest up and your elbows tight to your sides, curl the rope up until your hands are at chin height.
- Pause and hold this top position and squeeze your biceps to keep the tension on them.
- Slowly return to the start position, without letting your elbows move away from your sides at any point.
- At the bottom position,flex your triceps.

3B CABLE TRICEPS PRESS-DOWN

Sets 3 Reps 12 Tempo 2011 Rest 60sec
TARGETS Triceps

TOP TIP
Keep your back straight and don't "round" your shoulders. Your torso should stay upright with only your arms moving.

FORM GUIDE

- Stand tall in front of a cable machine with your chest up and core engaged, using both hands to hold a double rope handle attached to the high pulley.
- Keeping your chest up and your elbows tight to your sides, press your hands down until your arms are fully straight.
- Pause and hold this bottom position and flex your triceps to keep the tension on them.
- Slowly return to the start position, without letting your elbows move away from your sides at any point.
- At the top position, squeeze your biceps.

WEEK 3 **SESSION 4**

SHOULDERS AND ABS	SETS	REPS	TEMPO	REST
1A Dumbbell shoulder press	4	10	2010	30sec
1B Dumbbell lateral raise	4	10	2011	60sec
2A Cable cross-over	3	12	2011	30sec
2B Cable face pull	3	12	2011	60sec
3A Weighted crunch reach	3	12	1111	30sec
3B Weighted seated Russian twist	3	12	1111	60sec

1A DUMBBELL SHOULDER PRESS

Sets 4 Reps 10 Tempo 2010 Rest 30sec
TARGETS Shoulders, triceps

TOP TIP
If you start to struggle near the end of a set, bend your knees and then stand back up to initiate the final reps.

FORM GUIDE

- Stand tall with your chest up and core braced, holding a dumbbell in each hand at shoulder height with your palms facing forwards.
- Keeping your chest up and abs engaged, press the weights directly overhead until your arms are straight and the weights touch above your head.
- Slowly lower the weights back to the start position under complete control and keep each rep smooth without any bouncing.

1B DUMBBELL LATERAL RAISE

Sets 4 Reps 10 Tempo 2011 Rest 60sec
TARGETS Side shoulders

TOP TIP
At the top position your elbows should be the highest part of your arm so your side delts are doing all the work.

FORM GUIDE

- Stand tall with your chest up, abs braced and feet hip-width apart, holding a light dumbbell in each hand by your sides with your palms facing one another.
- Lean forwards slightly from the hips and, keeping a slight bend in your elbows, raise the weights out to the sides, no higher than shoulder height.
- As the weights approach shoulder height, rotate your wrists slightly so that your little fingers are pointing up to the ceiling to contract your side delts harder.
- Pause and hold this top position for a second, then slowly lower the weights under complete control.

2A CABLE CROSS-OVER

Sets 3 Reps 12 Tempo 2011 Rest 30sec
TARGETS Chest

TOP TIP
Don't allow your arms to "swing" back to the start – it will place huge pressure on your joints and your chest muscles.

FORM GUIDE

- Stand tall with a split stance in the middle of a cable machine, holding a D-handle in each hand attached to the high pulley.
- Keeping your chest up, core braced and a slight bend in your elbows, bring your hands down in a smooth arc to meet in front of your hips.
- Hold this bottom position for one second, squeezing your chest muscles hard, then reverse the movement back to the start.

2B CABLE FACE PULL

Sets 3 Reps 12 Tempo 2011 Rest 60sec
TARGETS Rear shoulders, upper back

TOP TIP
Protect your delicate shoulder joints by using a light weight and keeping each rep smooth and controlled.

FORM GUIDE

- Stand tall in front of a cable machine holding a double-rope handle in both hands, with thumbs closest to you.
- Keeping your chest up and abs engaged, stand so that there is tension in the cable when your arms are straight.
- Bring your hands up and to the sides of your head, so that your upper arms and forearms form right angles, and your upper arm is parallel to the floor.
- Pause and hold this top position for one second, squeezing your upper back and rear delts, then reverse the movement to the start position.

3A WEIGHTED CRUNCH REACH

Sets 3 Reps 12 Tempo 1111 Rest 30sec
TARGETS Upper abs

TOP TIP
Maintain a tight core from the start of the first rep to the end of the set – this will develop your abs much faster.

FORM GUIDE

- Lie flat on your back with your knees bent, holding a dumbbell, weight plate or other resistance equipment in both hands with your arms straight.
- Engage your upper abs to initiate the rep and raise your upper back off the floor.
- Use your abs to crunch upwards, keeping your arms straight and raising the weight as high as you can.
- Pause and hold this top position, the slowly lower your torso back to the start.

3B WEIGHTED SEATED RUSSIAN TWIST

Sets 3 Reps 12 Tempo 1111 Rest 60sec
TARGETS Upper and side abs

TOP TIP
Keep your head up and in line with your torso as it rotates to the sides and maintain a steady rhythm for each rep.

FORM GUIDE

- Sit on the floor with your knees bent and feet slightly raised, holding a dumbbell, weight plate or other resistance equipment in both hands with elbows bent.
- Engage your abs and, keeping your entire core tight, twist your torso to one side, leading with the weight, then twist back all the way round to the other side, then back to the middle. That's one rep.
- Make each rep harder by keeping your lower abs engaged and preventing your feet from touching the floor until the set is over.

WEEK 4 SESSION 1

CHEST AND BACK	SETS	REPS	TEMPO	REST
1A Incline dumbbell hammer press	4	12	2010	30sec
1B Dumbbell prone row	4	12	2011	60sec
2A Machine chest press	3	15	2010	30sec
2B Wide lat pull-down	3	15	2011	60sec
3A Cable flye	3	15	2011	30sec
3B Cable straight-arm pull-down	3	15	2011	60sec

WEEK 4 **SESSION 2**

LEGS AND ABS	SETS	REPS	TEMPO	REST
1A Front squat	4	12	2010	30sec
1B Romanian deadlift	4	12	2010	60sec
2A Leg extension	3	15	2011	30sec
2B Hamstring curl	3	15	2011	60sec
3A Hanging knee raise	3	15	1111	30sec
3B Hanging knee twist	3	15	1111	60sec

WEEK 4 **SESSION 3**

BICEPS AND TRICEPS	SETS	REPS	TEMPO	REST
1A Incline close-grip bench press	4	12	2010	30sec
1B Underhand lat pull-down	4	12	2011	60sec
2A Standing EZ-bar biceps curl	3	15	2011	30sec
2B Lying EZ-bar triceps extension	3	15	2011	60sec
3A Cable hammer curl	3	15	2011	30sec
3B Cable triceps press-down	3	15	2011	60sec

WEEK 4 **SESSION 4**

SHOULDERS AND ABS	SETS	REPS	TEMPO	REST
1A Dumbbell shoulder press	4	12	2010	30sec
1B Dumbbell lateral raise	4	12	2011	60sec
2A Cable cross-over	3	15	2011	30sec
2B Cable face pull	3	15	2011	60sec
3A Weighted crunch reach	3	15	1111	30sec
3B Weighted seated Russian twist	3	15	1111	60sec

B3.

You're now halfway through the New Body Plan, with four weeks of solid training under your increasingly loose-fitting belt. The workouts so far have been based on building first strength and then size, and you should also have noticed significant changes to how you look in the bathroom mirror.

With four weeks left, now's the time to ramp up the fat-burning focus with the introduction of end-of-session cardio drills while still adding lean muscle mass so you make greater strides towards building a stronger, leaner body. Turn the page to discover how this block of the plan works and how to execute each session perfectly.

GET LEAN IN BLOCK 3

You're now halfway through your eight-week New Body Plan, and in this block the focus shifts to burning body fat faster so you look bigger and leaner

GOAL

SPLIT

STRUCTURE

PROGRESSION

The goal in this penultimate block of the plan is to accelerate the speed at which your body burns fat. Having spent the first block getting stronger, and the second getting bigger, now's the time to increase your body's fat-burning capabilities to move you a huge step closer to achieving that bigger, stronger and leaner physique you want. To make that happen, in this block we introduce "finishers" at the end of each of the sessions. These are high-intensity interval training (HIIT) drills that'll send your heart rate soaring to dramatically increase calorie expenditure.

The muscles that you'll work in each session in this block have changed. In the first session of both weeks you'll work your chest and triceps; in the second, your legs and abs; in the third, your back and biceps; and in the fourth session, your shoulders and abs. This approach uses the concept of complementary supersets, which is the lideal approach for training multiple muscles groups that work together more effectively. You'll fatigue more muscle fibres and increase your heart rate to get both a muscle-building and fat-burning effect.

As with previous blocks, there are four sessions a week, but another big change to accelerate your progress is that each workout contains eight moves: seven resistance-based exercises and the HIIT finisher. Each workout begins with a straight set of a big compound lift to fire up your muscles and central nervous system. Then there are three complementary supersets to work the target muscles as thoroughly as possible. Each session ends with a finisher, and what to do and how to do it is described in detail on that session's workout pages.

The second week of the block uses the same body part split and the same exercises in the same order as the first, but with one major difference. For the first straight set move you'll do a total of five sets, up from four, and for the final superset (moves 4A and 4B) you'll do a total of three sets, up from two. On paper that might not seem a big change, but it's a significant increase in workload to push your muscles harder, and consequently increase how hard your heart and lungs must work during the finisher. This increase in effort and energy expenditure will again accelerate your fat-loss progress.

WEEK 5 **SESSION 1**

CHEST AND TRICEPS	SETS	REPS	TEMPO	REST
1 Decline bench press	4	8	2010	60sec
2A Cable flye	4	10	2011	30sec
2B Cable triceps press-down	4	10	2011	60sec
3A Lying EZ-bar triceps extension	3	10	2011	30sec
3B Lying EZ-bar triceps press	3	20	2011	60sec
4A Press-up	2	15	2010	30sec
4B Tall plank shoulder tap	2	20	1111	60sec
5 FINISHER Prowler push	1	10	X	60sec

1 DECLINE BENCH PRESS

Sets 4 Reps 8 Tempo 2010 Rest 60sec

TARGETS Chest, triceps, front shoulders

FORM GUIDE

- Lie on a decline bench with a wider than shoulder-width overhand grip on the bar with straight arms.
- Brace your core and back muscles.
- Keeping your whole body tight and your chest up, lower the bar towards your chest under complete control.
- Lower the bar until it touches your chest, then press it back up to the start position.
- Don't "bounce" the bar on your chest.

2A CABLE FLYE

Sets 4 Reps 10 Tempo 2011 Rest 30sec

TARGETS Chest

FORM GUIDE

- Stand tall with a split stance in the middle of a cable machine, holding a D-handle in each hand attached to the high pulley.
- Keeping your chest up, core braced, and a slight bend in your elbows, bring your hands down in a smooth arc to meet in front of your chest.
- Hold this position, squeezing your chest muscles hard, then reverse the movement to the start.

2B CABLE TRICEPS PRESS-DOWN

Sets 4 Reps 10 Tempo 2011 Rest 60sec

TARGETS Triceps, lower chest

FORM GUIDE

- Stand tall with your chest up in front of a cable machine holding a double rope handle in both hands.
- Keeping your chest up and your elbows at your sides, press your hands down until your arms are fully straight.
- Pause and flex your triceps to keep the tension on them.
- Slowly return to the start position.

3A LYING EZ-BAR TRICEPS EXTENSION

Sets **3** Reps **10** Tempo **2011** Rest **30sec**
TARGETS Triceps

FORM GUIDE

- Lie on a flat bench, holding an EZ-bar above your chest with straight arms.
- Keeping your elbows locked in position, pointing to the ceiling, slowly lower the bar towards the top of your head by bending your elbows.
- Without arching your back, slowly return the bar to the start position by straightening your arms.

TOP TIP
To work your triceps properly, your elbows shouldn't move. If they do, halt the set and reduce the weight.

3B LYING EZ-BAR TRICEPS PRESS

Sets **3** Reps **20** Tempo **2011** Rest **60sec**
TARGETS Triceps, chest

FORM GUIDE

- Lie on a flat bench, holding an EZ-bar above your chest with straight arms.
- Slowly lower the bar to your chest, keeping your elbows close to your sides and not allowing them to flare out.
- Once the bar touches your chest, press it back up to the start powerfully, without bouncing it back up off your chest.

TOP TIP
Use the same weight for this move as you used for move 3A. Rest lying on the bench in the start position after 3A.

4A PRESS-UP

Sets 2 Reps 15 Tempo 2010 Rest 30sec

TARGETS Chest, triceps, front shoulders

FORM GUIDE

- Get into the press-up position with your body in a straight line.
- Raise your hips and brace your core to keep your entire body stable.
- Bend your elbows to lower your chest towards the floor, but don't let them flare out – they should stay tight to your sides.
- Go as low as you can, then press back up to straighten your arms and return to the start position.

4B TALL PLANK SHOULDER TAP

Sets 2 Reps 20 Tempo 1111 Rest 60sec

TARGETS Triceps, front shoulders, abs

FORM GUIDE

- Get into position with your palms on the floor, your wrists underneath your shoulders and your body in a straight line from head to heels.
- Keep your abs and glutes engaged to hold this position without letting your hips sag.
- Lift one hand off the floor and tap your opposite shoulder. Return it and repeat with your other hand. That's one rep.

5 FINISHER PROWLER PUSH

Sets 1 Reps 10 Tempo X Rest 60sec

TARGETS Fat loss

FORM GUIDE

- Stand in front of a track – ideally 10m long – in front of a prowler bar loaded with around half your bodyweight.
- Grip the poles tightly halfway up. Keeping your core tight, drive through your legs to push the prowler forwards.
- At the end, turn around and come back. That's one rep. Rest for 30sec then repeat for a total of ten reps.

WEEK 5 **SESSION 2**

LEGS AND ABS	SETS	REPS	TEMPO	REST
1 Leg press	4	12	2010	60sec
2A Leg extension	4	10	2011	30sec
2B Hamstring curl	4	10	2011	60sec
3A Bodyweight squat	3	20	2110	30sec
3B Jump squat	3	10	X	60sec
4A Gym ball weighted crunch reach	2	15	1111	30sec
4B Plank toe tap	2	20	1111	60sec
5 FINISHER Farmer's walk	1	10	X	60sec

1 LEG PRESS

Sets 4 Reps 12 Tempo 2010 Rest 60sec

TARGETS Quads, hamstrings, glutes

FORM GUIDE

- Adjust the machine so when you sit on it you're positioned correctly and safely.
- Your feet should be hip-width apart with your toes pointing slightly outwards, and your knees bent.
- Push through your heels to straighten your legs without fully locking your knees at the top, then bend them again to return to the start position.

2A LEG EXTENSION

Sets 4 Reps 10 Tempo 2011 Rest 30sec

TARGETS Quads

FORM GUIDE

- Prepare the machine so when you sit on it you're positioned correctly and safely.
- Raise the bar by raising your feet until both legs are fully straight.
- Hold this top position for one second, keeping the maximum amount of tension on your quads, then slowly lower your feet back to the start position.

2B HAMSTRING CURL

Sets 4 Reps 10 Tempo 2010 Rest 60sec

TARGETS Hamstrings

FORM GUIDE

- Prepare the machine so when you sit on it you're positioned correctly and safely.
- Lower the bar by bending your knees and pulling your feet down underneath your body.
- Hold this bottom position for one second, keeping the maximum amount of tension on your hamstrings, then return to the start.

3A BODYWEIGHT SQUAT

Sets 3 Reps 20 Tempo 2110 Rest 30sec

TARGETS Quads, hamstrings, glutes, abs

TOP TIP
Don't "bounce" out of the bottom position. Try pausing there for a second to maintain muscular tension.

FORM GUIDE

- Stand tall with your chest up, abs engaged and arms straight by your sides.
- Bend your knees to squat down as low as you can, either keeping your arms by your sides or raising them up to shoulder height.
- Push through your heels to straighten your legs and return to the start position.

3B JUMP SQUAT

Sets 3 Reps 10 Tempo X Rest 60sec

TARGETS Quads, hamstrings, glutes, abs

TOP TIP
The X for the tempo means perform each rep explosively. Keep reps fast but land softly on your feet after each one.

FORM GUIDE

- Stand tall with your chest up, abs engaged and arms straight by your sides.
- Bend your knees to squat down and swing your arms backwards.
- Push through your heels to straighten your legs and jump powerfully off the floor.
- Land on both feet and go straight into the next rep.

4A GYM BALL WEIGHTED CRUNCH REACH

Sets 2 Reps 15 Tempo 1111 Rest 30sec
TARGETS Upper abs

FORM GUIDE

- Lie with your upper back on a gym ball, holding a dumbbell or weight plate in both hands with your arms straight.
- Use your abs to crunch upwards, keeping your arms straight and raising the weight as high as you can.
- Pause and hold this top position, then slowly lower your torso back to the start.

4B PLANK TOE TAP

Sets 2 Reps 20 Tempo 1111 Rest 60sec
TARGETS Core

FORM GUIDE

- Get into a plank, supporting yourself on your forearms with your elbows underneath your shoulders.
- Engage your abs, then raise your hips so that your body forms a straight line.
- Without letting your hips sag, lift one foot out as far as you can to the side. Tap your toe down on the floor, then bring it back in and repeat with the other foot. That's one rep.

5 FINISHER FARMER'S WALK

Sets 1 Reps 10 Tempo X Rest 60sec
TARGETS Fat loss

FORM GUIDE

- Stand in front of a long, clear track – ideally at least 10m long – holding a trap bar deadlift bar, dumbbells or specialist farmer's walk equipment.
- Keeping your core braced, walk the length of the track.
- At the end, turn around and walk back to the start. That's one rep. Rest for 30sec then repeat for a total of ten reps.

WEEK 5 **SESSION 3**

BACK AND BICEPS	SETS	REPS	TEMPO	REST
1 Rack deadlift	4	8	2011	60sec
2A Wide lat pull-down	4	10	2011	30sec
2B Underhand lat pull-down	4	12	2011	60sec
3A Dumbbell prone row	3	10	2011	30sec
3B EZ-bar prone spider curl	3	12	2011	60sec
4A Seated dumbbell biceps curl	2	15	2011	30sec
4B Seated dumbbell hammer curl	2	15	2011	60sec
5 FINISHER SkiErg or rower	10	100m	X	30sec

1 RACK DEADLIFT

Sets 4 Reps 8 Tempo 2011 Rest 60sec
TARGETS Back

FORM GUIDE

- Position a barbell in front of you raised on blocks or at knee height on safety bars in a squat rack.
- Bend at the knees and hips to hold the bar with a wide overhand grip.
- Grip the bar hard then, pushing through your heels, stand up, pushing your hips forwards and retracting your shoulder blades at the top.
- Reverse the move back to the start.

2A WIDE LAT PULL-DOWN

Sets 4 Reps 10 Tempo 2011 Rest 30sec
TARGETS Lats

FORM GUIDE

- Adjust the machine so you're sitting with your knees secured with a wide overhand grip on the bar.
- Keeping your chest up and abs braced, pull the bar down, leading with your elbows.
- Hold the bottom position for a second, squeezing your biceps and back hard, then reverse the movement back to the start.

2B UNDERHAND LAT PULL-DOWN

Sets 4 Reps 12 Tempo 2011 Rest 60sec
TARGETS Lats, biceps

FORM GUIDE

- Adjust the machine so you're sitting with your knees secured with a narrow underhand grip on the bar.
- Keeping your chest up and abs braced, pull the bar down, leading with your elbows.
- Hold the bottom position for a second, squeezing your biceps and back hard, then reverse the movement back to the start.

3A DUMBBELL PRONE ROW

Sets 3 Reps 10 Tempo 2011 Rest 30sec
TARGETS Back, biceps

TOP TIP
Your chest must remain in contact with the bench so your back muscles, and not momentum, move the weights.

FORM GUIDE

- Lie chest-first on an incline bench, holding a dumbbell in each hand with a neutral grip and straight arms.
- Keeping your chest against the bench, row the weights up, leading with your elbows.
- At the top position pause and hold, squeezing your upper back hard, then slowly lower the weights back to the start.

3B EZ-BAR PRONE SPIDER CURL

Sets 3 Reps 12 Tempo 2011 Rest 60sec
TARGETS Biceps

TOP TIP
Remember to fully flex your triceps at the bottom of each rep to work your biceps through a full range.

FORM GUIDE

- Lie chest-first on an incline bench, holding an EZ-bar in both hands with straight arms.
- Keeping your chest against the bench, curl the bar up until your forearms go past horizontal.
- Hold the top position, squeezing your biceps hard, then lower the bar back to the start.

4A SEATED DUMBBELL BICEPS CURL

Sets 2 Reps 15 Tempo 2011 Rest 30sec
TARGETS Biceps

FORM GUIDE

- Sit on an upright bench, holding a dumbbell in each hand with your palms facing forwards.
- Keeping your elbows tight to your sides, curl the dumbbells up towards your shoulders.
- At the top position, pause and squeeze your biceps hard, then slowly lower the weights.
- Fully straighten your arm and flex your triceps at the bottom position.

4B SEATED DUMBBELL HAMMER CURL

Sets 2 Reps 15 Tempo 2011 Rest 60sec
TARGETS Biceps

FORM GUIDE

- Sit on an upright bench, holding a dumbbell in each hand with your palms facing your sides.
- Keeping your elbows tight to your sides, curl the dumbbells up towards your shoulders.
- At the top position, pause and squeeze your biceps hard, then slowly lower the weights.
- Fully straighten your arm and flex your triceps at the bottom position.

5 FINISHER SKIERG OR ROWER

Sets 10 Reps 100m Tempo X Rest 30sec
TARGETS Fat Loss

FORM GUIDE

- Using either a SkiErg or rowing machine, position yourself in the correct start position. Set the display to show metres travelled.
- Row hard for 100m, keeping each stroke fast but controlled, then rest for 30sec.
- Repeat this ten times until you have covered 1km.

WEEK 5 SESSION 4

SHOULDERS AND ABS	SETS	REPS	TEMPO	REST
1 Overhead press	4	12	2010	60sec
2A Seated dumbbell shoulder press	4	10	2010	30sec
2B Seated dumbbell lateral raise	4	12	2011	60sec
3A Cable reverse flye	3	10	2011	30sec
3B Cable face pull	3	12	2011	60sec
4A Kettlebell halo	2	8	1111	30sec
4B Kettlebell plank drag	2	12	1111	60sec
5 FINISHER Kettlebell swing	4	25	X	60sec

1 OVERHEAD PRESS

Sets 4 Reps 12 Tempo 2010 Rest 60sec

TARGETS Shoulders, triceps

FORM GUIDE

- With your feet shoulder-width apart, hold a bar on your upper chest, with hands just wider than shoulder-width apart.
- Keeping your chest up, and abs and glutes engaged, press the bar up until your arms are straight.
- Slowly lower the bar back to the start, then repeat the move without "bouncing" it back up off your shoulders.

2A SEATED DUMBBELL SHOULDER PRESS

Sets 4 Reps 10 Tempo 2010 Rest 30sec

TARGETS Shoulders, triceps

FORM GUIDE

- Sit on an upright bench holding a dumbbell in each hand at shoulder-height with your palms facing away from you. Plant your feet on the floor.
- Keeping your chest up and abs engaged, press the weights directly overhead until your arms are straight and the weights touch above your head.
- Slowly lower the weights back to the start position.

2B SEATED DUMBBELL LATERAL RAISE

Sets 4 Reps 12 Tempo 2011 Rest 60sec

TARGETS Side shoulders

FORM GUIDE

- Sit on an upright bench holding a light dumbbell in each hand by your sides.
- Keeping a slight bend in your elbows, raise the weights to shoulder height.
- As the weights approach shoulder height, rotate your wrists so that your little fingers are pointing up to the ceiling.
- Pause and hold this top position, then slowly lower the weights.

3A CABLE REVERSE FLYE

Sets 3 Reps 10 Tempo 2011 Rest 30sec

TARGETS Rear shoulders, upper back

FORM GUIDE

- Stand tall in front of a cable machine with your arms crossed holding a D-handle, attached to the low pulley, in each hand.
- Keeping your back straight and with a slight bend in your elbows, raise your hands out to the sides.
- Pause and hold this top position for one second, squeezing your upper back and rear delts, then reverse the movement back to the start position.

3B CABLE FACE PULL

Sets 3 Reps 12 Tempo 2011 Rest 60sec

TARGETS Rear shoulders, upper back

FORM GUIDE

- Stand tall in front of a cable machine holding a double-rope handle in both hands, with thumbs closest to you.
- Keeping your chest up and abs engaged, stand so that there is tension in the cable when you arms are straight.
- Bring your hands up and to the sides of your head, so that your upper arms and forearms form right angles, and so your upper arm is parallel to the floor.
- Pause and hold this top position for one second, squeezing your upper back and rear delts, then reverse the movement back to the start position.

4A KETTLEBELL HALO

Sets 2 Reps 8 Tempo 1111 Rest 30sec
TARGETS Abs, obliques, shoulders

FORM GUIDE

- Stand tall with your chest up, holding a kettlebell by the handle with both hands.
- Brace your abs, then lift the bell and manoeuvre it around your head, bending your elbows as it passes behind you for the maximum range of motion.
- Each full rotation counts as one rep.
- Move it clockwise in the first set, then anti-clockwise in the second.

4B KETTLEBELL PLANK DRAG

Sets 2 Reps 12 (6 each direction) Tempo 1111 Rest 60sec
TARGETS Chest, triceps

FORM GUIDE

- Get into a straight-arm plank position with your body in a straight line from head to heels and position a kettlebell to one side of your body.
- Reach under your body with the opposite hand to drag the bell across to the other side. That's one rep.
- Then move it back in the other direction, keeping your hips up and your entire core fully engaged throughout.

5 FINISHER KETTLEBELL SWING

Sets 4 Reps 25 Tempo X Rest 60sec
TARGETS Fat loss

FORM GUIDE

- Stand tall with your feet wider than shoulder-width apart, holding a kettlebell between your legs with both hands
- Pop your hips forwards to drive it up to head height, keeping your arms relaxed.
- Let the kettlebell swing back into the next rep – you don't need to bend your knees much.

WEEK 6 SESSION 1

CHEST AND TRICEPS	SETS	REPS	TEMPO	REST
1 Decline bench press	5	8	2010	60sec
2A Cable flye	4	10	2011	30sec
2B Cable triceps press-down	4	10	2011	60sec
3A Lying EZ-bar triceps extension	3	10	2011	30sec
3B Lying EZ-bar triceps press	3	20	2011	60sec
4A Press-up	3	15	2010	30sec
4B Tall plank shoulder tap	3	20	1111	60sec
5 FINISHER Prowler push	1	12	X	60sec

WEEK 6 **SESSION 2**

LEGS AND ABS	SETS	REPS	TEMPO	REST
1 Leg press	5	12	2010	60sec
2A Leg extension	4	10	2011	30sec
2B Hamstring curl	4	10	2011	60sec
3A Bodyweight squat	3	20	2110	30sec
3B Jump squat	3	10	X	60sec
4A Gym ball weighted crunch reach	3	15	1111	30sec
4B Plank toe tap	3	20	1111	60sec
5 FINISHER Farmer's walk	1	12	X	60sec

WEEK 6 **SESSION 3**

BACK AND BICEPS	SETS	REPS	TEMPO	REST
1 Rack deadlift	5	8	2011	60sec
2A Wide lat pull-down	4	10	2011	30sec
2B Underhand lat pull-down	4	12	2011	60sec
3A Dumbbell prone row	3	10	2011	30sec
3B EZ-bar prone spider curl	3	12	2011	60sec
4A Seated dumbbell biceps curl	3	15	2011	30sec
4B Seated dumbbell hammer curl	3	15	2011	60sec
5 FINISHER SkiErg or rower	10	200m	X	60sec

WEEK 6 **SESSION 4**

SHOULDERS AND ABS	SETS	REPS	TEMPO	REST
1 Overhead press	5	12	2010	60sec
2A Seated dumbbell shoulder press	4	10	2010	30sec
2B Seated dumbbell lateral raise	4	12	2011	60sec
3A Cable reverse flye	3	10	2011	30sec
3B Cable face pull	3	12	2011	60sec
4A Kettlebell halo	3	8	1111	30sec
4B Kettlebell plank drag	3	12	1111	60sec
5 FINISHER Kettlebell swing	6	25	X	60sec

It's the final block of the plan and by now you should have noticed some major changes to your body, with more lean muscle mass and less body fat, and be feeling fitter and healthier.

And because you're now stronger and fitter it means you can push even harder in this critical final block to end your New Body Plan journey looking and feeling better than you ever thought possible. The sessions are now geared towards increasing your calorie expenditure while also providing the precise training stimulus to keep building new muscle tissue. Turn the page to read how you can finish the plan strongly to put the finishing touches to your best ever body.

GET RIPPED IN BLOCK 4

By now you'll look and feel noticeably bigger and leaner, so it's time to step it up for the final two weeks to torch those last stubborn bits of body fat

GOAL

SPLIT

STRUCTURE

PROGRESSION

In this final two-week block the entire focus is on building more lean muscle mass while stripping away as much fat as possible. If you have followed the workouts to the letter you will already significantly look and – just as importantly – feel bigger, stronger and leaner than when you started, and we'll bet you're now getting asked lots of questions about what you've done and how you've done it. But the time for talking will come; now's the time for action! Keep doing what you've been doing and give every session everything you've got to end this programme looking and feeling fantastic.

In Block 4 the workout split has again changed to give you the best possible odds of finishing the plan bigger and leaner than ever. For the first session of both weeks you'll work your chest. In the second you'll train your back and abs, in the third your biceps and triceps, and in the fourth your shoulders and abs. There isn't a dedicated legs session in this block, and that's for one simple reason: to allow your legs to be as fresh as possible so you can attack the finisher at the end of every session. These have been selected to work your legs hard, as well as your heart and lungs to burn fat.

While there are still four sessions a week, the number of moves in each workout changes depending on the muscle group or groups being worked. Every session starts with two straight sets of a big compound exercise, and then you'll do either one or two advanced supersets, where you work the same muscle group with back-to-back moves that will fatigue the target muscles completely. There's even a tri-set – which is three moves done in succession – in the back and abs session that works your entire abdominal region to bring out some definition to your abs.

In the first week of this block you'll do five sets of the first two exercises, then three sets of all subsequent moves. In the second week the number of sets of the first two moves stays at five, but you'll do an additional set of all other moves, bringing the total to four. As in the previous block there is a HIIT finisher at the end of every session to work your quads, hamstrings, glutes and abs, and to get – and keep – your heart rate high because that's what's going to burn off those final bits of stubborn body fat.

WEEK 7 **SESSION 1**

CHEST	SETS	REPS	TEMPO	REST
1 Bench press	5	10	2010	60sec
2 Cable cross-over	5	12	2011	60sec
3A Incline dumbbell bench press	3	15	2010	30sec
3B Incline dumbbell flye	3	15	2011	60sec
4 Press-up	3	15	2010	60sec
5 FINISHER Farmer's walk + kettlebell swing	1	8	X	60sec

1 BENCH PRESS

Sets 5 Reps 10 Tempo 2010 Rest 60sec
TARGETS Chest, triceps, front shoulders

TOP TIP
If you are lifting heavy ask a fellow gym-goer to "spot" you for the last couple of sets in case you need assistance.

FORM GUIDE

- Lie on a flat bench, holding a barbell with a wider than shoulder-width overhand grip. Plant your feet on the floor directly underneath your knees.
- Brace your core and back muscles, and press your feet into the ground.
- Keeping your whole body tight and your chest up, lower the bar until it touches your chest around nipple-level.
- Press the bar back up powerfully to straighten your arms and return to the start position.
- Don't "bounce" the bar on your chest at the bottom of a rep to help initiate the next one.

2 CABLE CROSS-OVER

Sets 5 Reps 12 Tempo 2011 Rest 60sec
TARGETS Chest, front shoulders

TOP TIP
Add greater definition to the middle of your chest by turning your wrists inwards as your hands meet in front of you.

FORM GUIDE

- Stand tall with a split stance in the middle of a cable machine, holding a D-handle in each hand attached to the high pulley.
- Keeping your chest up, core braced, and a slight bend in your elbows, bring your hands down in a smooth arc to meet in front of your hips.
- Hold this bottom position for one second, squeezing your chest muscles hard, then reverse the movement back to the start.

3A INCLINE DUMBBELL BENCH PRESS

Sets **3** Reps **15** Tempo **2010** Rest **30sec**

TARGETS Chest, triceps, front shoulders

TOP TIP
To get to the start position, lift the weights by resting them on your thighs, then move them up one knee at a time.

FORM GUIDE

- Lie on an incline bench holding a dumbbell in each hand at chest height. Plant your feet on the floor directly underneath your knees.
- Brace your core and back muscles, and press your feet into the ground.
- Keeping your whole body tight and your chest up, press the weights directly up until your arms are straight and the weights touch over the middle of your chest.
- Slowly lower the weights back to the start position under complete control.

3B INCLINE DUMBBELL FLYE

Sets **3** Reps **15** Tempo **2011** Rest **60sec**

TARGETS Chest

TOP TIP
Your shoulder joints are heavily involved in this move, so use light dumbbells to avoid overstraining them.

FORM GUIDE

- Lie on an incline bench, holding a dumbbell in each hand directly above your chest with straight arms. Plant your feet on the floor directly underneath your knees.
- With a slight bend in your elbows, lower the weights to the sides until you feel a good stretch across your upper chest.
- Squeeze your chest muscles to raise the weights back to the start position.

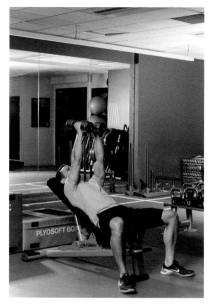

4 PRESS-UP

Sets 3 Reps 15 Tempo 2010 Rest 60sec
TARGETS Chest, triceps, front shoulders

TOP TIP
Don't fully straighten your arms at the top. Keep a slight bend in your elbows to maintain tension on your chest.

FORM GUIDE

- Get on all fours with your legs and arms straight, your hands under your shoulders and your body in a straight line from head to heels.
- Raise your hips and brace your core to keep your entire body stable.
- Bend your elbows to lower your chest towards the floor, but don't let them flare out – they should stay tight to your sides.
- Go as low as you can, then press back up to return to the start position.

5 FINISHER FARMER'S WALK + KB SWING

Sets 1 Reps 8 Tempo X Rest 60sec
TARGETS Fat Loss

TOP TIP
If your form breaks down, stop that rep and take a breather before continuing. Injuries are the enemy of getting lean.

FORM GUIDE

- Stand in front of a long, clear track – ideally at least 10m long – holding dumbbells or farmer's walk equipment.
- Keeping your core braced, walk down the length of the track.
- At the end, turn around and walk back to the start, then drop the weights and pick up a kettlebell.
- Stand tall with your feet wider than shoulder-width apart, holding a kettlebell between your legs with both hands, then pop your hips forwards to drive it up to head height, keeping your arms relaxed.
- Let the kettlebell swing back into the next rep. Do ten swings in total.
- Those two drills together count as one rep. Rest 60sec, then repeat.

WEEK 8 SESSION 2

BACK AND ABS	SETS	REPS	TEMPO	REST
1 Wide lat pull-down	5	10	2011	60sec
2 Seated row	5	12	2011	60sec
3A Cable straight-arm pull-down	3	12	2011	30sec
3B Cable face pull	3	15	2011	60sec
4A Hanging leg raise	3	12	1111	0sec
4B Hanging knee raise	3	12	1111	0sec
4C Hanging knee raise twist	3	12	1111	60sec
5 FINISHER Prowler push and drag	1	8	X	60sec

1 WIDE LAT PULL-DOWN

Sets 5 Reps 10 Tempo 2011 Rest 60sec
TARGETS Back, biceps

FORM GUIDE

- Position yourself on the machine with a double shoulder-width overhand grip on the bar.
- Keeping your chest up, abs braced and back straight, pull the bar down to chin height, leading with your elbows.
- Hold the bottom position for a second, squeezing your lats hard, then reverse the movement back to the start.

2 SEATED ROW

Sets 5 Reps 12 Tempo 2011 Rest 60sec
TARGETS Chest, triceps

FORM GUIDE

- Position yourself on the machine with your feet against the foot rest, holding a double-grip cable attachment in both hands.
- Keeping your chest up, back straight and core braced, row your hands in towards your body, leading with your elbows.
- Pause and squeeze your back and biceps muscles hard, then reverse the move back to the start position.

3A CABLE STRAIGHT-ARM PULL-DOWN

Sets 3 Reps 12 Tempo 2011 Rest 30sec
TARGETS Back

FORM GUIDE

- Stand tall, holding a straight-bar handle attached to the high pulley in both hands with straight arms.
- Bend forwards slightly from the hips and, keeping your chest up and arms straight, pull the bar down in a smooth arc so it hits your thighs.
- Hold this bottom position for one second, squeezing your lats hard, then reverse back to the start.

3B CABLE FACE PULL

Sets 3 Reps 15 Tempo 2011 Rest 60sec
TARGETS Back, rear shoulders

TOP TIP
Make sure the pulley is set no higher than head height to allow you to pull back while keeping your elbows up.

FORM GUIDE

- Stand tall in front of a cable machine holding a double-rope handle in both hands, with thumbs closest to you.
- Keeping your chest up and abs engaged, stand so that there is tension in the cable when you arms are straight.
- Bring your hands up and to the sides of your head, so that your upper arms and forearms form right angles, and your upper arm is parallel to the floor.
- Pause and hold this top position for one second, squeezing your upper back and rear delts, then reverse the movement back to the start position.

4A HANGING LEG RAISE

Sets 3 Reps 12 Tempo 1111 Rest 0sec
TARGETS Core, lower abs

TOP TIP
Holding your breath is tempting but sends your blood pressure soaring. Keep breathing with short, quick breaths.

FORM GUIDE

- Position yourself in the machine, or hang from a bar with a shoulder-width overhand grip and straight legs.
- Brace your core and glutes and, with your feet together, raise your legs until they are parallel to the floor.
- Hold this position for a second, then lower your legs back to the start position, keeping them straight.

4B HANGING KNEE RAISE

Sets 3 Reps 12 Tempo 1111 Rest 0sec
TARGETS Core, lower abs

FORM GUIDE

- Position yourself in the machine, or hang from a bar with a shoulder-width overhand grip and straight legs.
- Brace your core and glutes and, with your feet together, draw your knees up towards your chest.
- Hold this position, then straighten your legs to return to the start.

4C HANGING KNEE RAISE TWIST

Sets 3 Reps 12 Tempo 1111 Rest 60sec
TARGETS Core, lower abs, side abs

FORM GUIDE

- Position yourself in the machine, or hang from a bar with a shoulder-width overhand grip and straight legs.
- Brace your core and glutes and, with your feet together, draw your knees up towards your chest then twist your knees to one side, pause, then twist them across to the other side.
- Twist them back to the middle, then straighten your legs to return to the start position. That's one rep.

5 FINISHER PROWLER PUSH AND DRAG

Sets 1 Reps 8 Tempo X Rest 60sec
TARGETS Fat Loss

FORM GUIDE

- Stand on a track – ideally 10m long – in front of a prowler bar loaded with around half of your bodyweight, with TRX handles attached to the end closest to your feet.
- Push the prowler to the other end, then pick up the TRX handles and drag it back to the start. That's one rep.
- Rest 60sec, then repeat.

WEEK 7 **SESSION 3**

BICEPS AND TRICEPS	SETS	REPS	TEMPO	REST
1 Underhand lat pull-down	5	10	2011	60sec
2 Close-grip bench press	5	12	2010	60sec
3A EZ-bar preacher curl	3	12	2011	30sec
3B Dumbbell hammer curl	3	15	2011	60sec
4A Cable overhead triceps extension	3	12	2011	30sec
4B Cable triceps press-down	3	15	2011	60sec
5 FINISHER Battle ropes	1	8	30sec	30sec

1 UNDERHAND LAT PULL-DOWN

Sets 5 Reps 10 Tempo 2011 Rest 60sec
TARGETS Biceps, back

FORM GUIDE

- Prepare the machine, following the instructions to make the necessary adjustments so when you sit on it you're positioned correctly and safely.
- In the start position you should be sat with your knees secured, holding a straight bar with a shoulder-width underhand grip.
- Keeping your chest up and abs braced, pull the bar down, leading with your elbows.
- Hold the bottom position for a second, squeezing your biceps and back hard, then reverse the movement back to the start.

2 CLOSE-GRIP BENCH PRESS

Sets 5 Reps 12 Tempo 2011 Rest 60sec
TARGETS Triceps, chest, front shoulders

FORM GUIDE

- Lie on a flat bench, holding a barbell with a shoulder-width overhand grip. Plant your feet on the floor directly underneath your knees.
- Brace your core and back muscles, and press your feet into the ground.
- Keeping your whole body tight, lower the bar until it touches your chest around nipple-level.
- Press the bar back up powerfully to straighten your arms and return to the start position.
- Don't "bounce" the bar on your chest at the bottom of a rep to help initiate the next one.

3A EZ-BAR PREACHER CURL

Sets 3 Reps 12 Tempo 2011 Rest 30sec

TARGETS Biceps

TOP TIP
Avoid rocking back and forth to generate momentum, which only serves to take tension off the biceps.

FORM GUIDE

- Sit or stand at a preacher bench, holding an EZ-bar with an underhand grip.
- Keeping your upper arms and elbows on the bench, curl the bar up towards your chin until your forearms are vertical.
- Pause at this top position for one second, squeezing your biceps hard.
- Lower the bar slowly and under complete control, fully straightening your arms at the bottom.

3B DUMBBELL HAMMER CURL

Sets 3 Reps 15 Tempo 2011 Rest 30sec

TARGETS Biceps, forearms

TOP TIP
This is a high-rep set, but don't lift too light. If it gets hard, start curling one arm at a time to get more rest between reps.

FORM GUIDE

- Stand tall with your chest up, core braced and shoulders back, holding a pair of dumbbells with your palms facing your sides.
- Keeping your elbows tight to your sides, curl the dumbbells up towards your shoulders.
- At the top position, pause and squeeze your biceps hard, then slowly lower the weights under complete control.
- Fully straighten your arm and flex your triceps at the bottom of each rep to ensure your biceps muscles move through a full range of motion.

4A CABLE OVERHEAD TRICEPS EXTENSION

Sets 3 Reps 12 Tempo 2011 Rest 30sec
TARGETS Triceps

FORM GUIDE

- Stand tall, holding a double-rope handle attached to the low pulley of a cable machine.
- Turn your back to the machine with your hands by your head.
- Keeping your elbows next to your head and pointing up, press the handles up and forwards to straighten your arms.
- Flex your triceps at the top of the move, then return to the start.

4B CABLE TRICEPS PRESS-DOWN

Sets 3 Reps 15 Tempo 2011 Rest 60sec
TARGETS Triceps

FORM GUIDE

- Stand tall with your chest up, holding in both hands a double rope handle attached to the high pulley.
- Keeping your elbows tight to your sides, press your hands down until your arms are fully straight.
- Hold this bottom position and flex your triceps.
- Slowly return to the start position, without letting your elbows move away from your sides.

5 FINISHER BATTLE ROPES

Sets 1 Reps 8 Tempo 30sec Rest 30sec
TARGETS Fat Loss

FORM GUIDE

- Stand upright with your feet hip-width apart, holding a battle rope in each hand.
- Move the ropes up and down at the same time, creating a wave movement through both ropes.
- Move the ropes quickly and smoothly for 45sec, keeping your chest up and your core tight. Rest 45sec and repeat.

NO ROPES?
If you don't have battle ropes, you can instead do 5 sets of 25 kettlebell swings, resting for 45 seconds between each set.

WEEK 7 **SESSION 4**

SHOULDERS AND ABS	SETS	REPS	TEMPO	REST
1 Dumbbell shoulder press	5	10	2010	60sec
2 EZ-bar upright row	5	12	2011	60sec
3A Seated Arnold press	3	12	2010	30sec
3B Seated dumbbell lateral raise	3	15	2011	60sec
4A Gym ball weighted crunch reach	3	15	1111	0sec
4B Gym ball weighted Russian twist	3	12	1111	60sec
5 Plank jack	3	25	X	60sec
6 FINISHER SkiErg or Rower + KB swing	1	8	X	60sec

1 DUMBBELL SHOULDER PRESS

Sets 5 Reps 10 Tempo 2010 Rest 60sec
TARGETS Shoulders, triceps

FORM GUIDE

- Stand tall with your chest up and core braced, holding a dumbbell in each hand at shoulder height with your palms facing away from you.
- Keeping your chest up and abs engaged, press the weights directly overhead until your arms are straight.
- Slowly lower the weights back to the start position under complete control.

2 EZ-BAR UPRIGHT ROW

Sets 5 Reps 12 Tempo 2011 Rest 60sec
TARGETS Traps, shoulders, biceps

FORM GUIDE

- Stand tall, holding an EZ-bar with an overhand shoulder-width grip.
- Keeping your chest up, row the bar upwards towards your chin, leading with your elbows.
- Pause and hold for one second in this top position, then slowly lower the bar until your arms are straight.

3A SEATED ARNOLD PRESS

Sets 3 Reps 12 Tempo 2010 Rest 30sec
TARGETS Shoulders, triceps

FORM GUIDE

- Sit on an upright bench holding a dumbbell in each hand at shoulder height with your palms facing you. Plant your feet on the floor.
- Keeping your chest up and abs engaged, press the weights directly overhead, rotating your wrists as you go so you finish with straight arms and your palms facing away.
- Reverse the move back to the start.

3B SEATED DUMBBELL LATERAL RAISE

Sets 3 Reps 15 Tempo 2011 Rest 60sec
TARGETS Side shoulders

FORM GUIDE

- Sit on an upright bench, holding a light dumbbell in each hand by your sides.
- Keeping a slight bend in your elbows, raise the weights to shoulder height.
- As the weights approach shoulder height, rotate your wrists so that your little fingers are pointing up to the ceiling.
- Pause and hold this top position, then slowly lower back to the start.

TOP TIP
Work your delts even harder by pausing each rep when your hands are 20cm from your body, then continuing the lift.

4A GYM BALL WEIGHTED CRUNCH REACH

Sets 3 Reps 15 Tempo 1111 Rest 0sec
TARGETS Upper abs, core

FORM GUIDE

- Lie with your upper back on a gym ball, holding a dumbbell or weight plate in both hands with your arms straight.
- Use your abs to crunch upwards, keeping your arms straight and raising the weight as high as you can.
- Pause and hold this top position for one second, then slowly lower your torso back to the start.

TOP TIP
Achieving a good contraction and hold in your upper abs is more important than weight in sculpting in a six-pack.

4B GYM BALL WEIGHTED RUSSIAN TWIST

Sets 3 Reps 12 Tempo 1111 Rest 0sec
TARGETS Upper abs, side abs, core

FORM GUIDE

- Lie with your upper back on a gym ball, holding a dumbbell or weight plate in both hands with your arms straight.
- Keeping your arms straight, rotate your torso to one side as low as you can go. Make sure your head follows the line of your arms.
- Reverse back to the start, then rotate to the other side. That's one rep. Keep your abs engaged throughout.

5 PLANK JACK

Sets 3 Reps 25 Tempo X Rest 60sec
TARGETS Abs, core

FORM GUIDE

- Get into the plank position and engage your abs and raise your hips so that your body forms a straight line.
- Without letting your hips sag, jump both feet out to the sides, then back in together – that's one rep.
- Keep your core and glutes engaged throughout.

6 FINISHER SKIERG OR ROWER + KB SWING

Sets 1 Reps 8 Tempo X Rest 60sec
TARGETS Fat Loss

FORM GUIDE

- Set the machine display to show metres travelled and row hard for 100m, then get off and pick up a kettlebell.
- Swing the bell to head height, keeping your arms relaxed.
- Let the kettlebell swing back into the next rep. Do ten swings in total.
- Those two drills together count as one rep. Rest 60sec, then repeat.

WEEK 8 SESSION 1

CHEST	SETS	REPS	TEMPO	REST
1 Bench press	5	10	2010	60sec
2 Cable cross-over	5	12	2011	60sec
3A Incline dumbbell bench press	4	15	2010	30sec
3B Incline dumbbell flye	4	15	2011	60sec
4 Press-up	4	15	2010	60sec
5 FINISHER Farmer's walk + KB swing	1	10	X	60sec

WEEK 8 **SESSION 2**

BACK AND ABS	SETS	REPS	TEMPO	REST
1 Wide lat pull-down	5	10	2011	60sec
2 Seated row	5	12	2011	60sec
3A Cable straight-arm pull-down	4	12	2011	30sec
3B Cable face pull	4	15	2011	60sec
4A Hanging leg raise	4	12	1111	0sec
4B Hanging knee raise	4	12	1111	0sec
4C Hanging knee raise twist	4	12	1111	60sec
5 FINISHER Prowler push and drag	1	10	X	60sec

WEEK 8 **SESSION 3**

BICEPS AND TRICEPS	SETS	REPS	TEMPO	REST
1 Underhand lat pull-down	5	10	2011	60sec
2 Close-grip bench press	5	12	2010	60sec
3A EZ-bar preacher curl	4	12	2011	30sec
3B Dumbbell hammer curl	4	15	2011	60sec
4A Cable overhead triceps extension	4	12	2011	30sec
4B Cable triceps press-down	4	15	2011	60sec
5 FINISHER Battle ropes	1	10	40sec	40sec

WEEK 8 **SESSION 4**

SHOULDERS AND ABS	SETS	REPS	TEMPO	REST
1 Dumbbell shoulder press	5	10	2010	60sec
2 EZ-bar upright row	5	12	2011	60sec
3A Seated Arnold press	4	12	2010	30sec
3B Seated dumbbell lateral raise	4	15	2011	60sec
4A Gym ball weighted crunch reach	4	15	1111	0sec
4B Gym ball weighted Russian twist	4	12	1111	60sec
5 Plank jack	4	25	X	60sec
6 FINISHER SkiErg or rower + KB swing	1	10	X	60sec

Every qualified trainer has said "you can't out-train a bad diet" at some point. To build your best ever body, you need a smart and sustainable nutrition plan as much as a challenging and progressive training plan. Lucky for you, eating for the bigger and leaner body you want has never been easier thanks to some new and unique approaches and strategies created for the New Body Plan.

Everything you need to know is explained over the following pages, so read on to find out how some very simple changes to what – and how – you eat can make a huge positive difference to how you look and feel.

THE SMART AND SIMPLE WAY TO EAT FOR A BETTER BODY

Some quick and easy tweaks to your daily diet are all it takes to kick-start the processes by which your body burns fat and builds muscle

When you're trying to build a bigger, stronger and leaner body, what and when you eat is as important as how you exercise because no-one ever built a better physique through training alone. In this chapter you'll learn about the best ways to eat to start burning fat and building muscle straight away, so you get your eight-week transformation off to the best possible start.

EAT YOUR WAY LEAN

First up are the basics: the seven rules you need to follow to start eating for a leaner and more muscular body. Then there's an in-depth look at the 90% Nutrition guide, which is a way of eating for a better body without having to give up or avoid your favourite foods. After all, telling yourself you can't have something is often the quickest way to make you start craving it – but the beauty of all the nutrition advice in this plan is that nothing is off the menu. It's all about moderation, so you can stay positive, focused and motivated to build a better body without worrying or obsessing over food.

Then there's all the information you need about the three major food groups – protein, fats, and carbs – and how each one plays an important role in your better-body aspirations, as well as all the essential vitamins and minerals you need to start looking and feeling great.

After that there's an explanation of the Perfect Portion approach to meal-building. This and the 90% Nutrition rule are the two guidelines that will keep you on the right track to move ever closer to your physique goal. Everything you need to know about how to build the perfect meal to suit

that goal – whether it's accelerating fat burn or maximising muscle building – is explained in full, but it couldn't be easier to understand and follow. You don't need kitchen scales or a calculator to count calories: all you need are your hands!

To finish off, there's a guide to how to improve your gut health so more of the nutrients you eat can be put to the best possible use, as well as making you look and feel healthier; suggestions about how you can be more mindful during mealtimes to foster a better relationship with food, so you enjoy it more and prevent overeating those foods you should be cutting back on; and a complete overview of those sports nutrition supplements that can accelerate your progress, both by improving gym focus and motivation and helping you recover faster.

EASY DOES IT

If you've ever tried to lose weight in the past but failed because you couldn't adhere to a boring diet, or found yourself very quickly craving those foods that you were "banned" from eating, following the New Body Plan nutrition guide is going to be a transformative experience in itself.

Following the advice, tips and guidelines over the coming pages will demonstrate once and for all that it's possible to lose significant amounts of body fat *and* build lean muscle while enjoying a rich and varied diet, and not having to forsake your favourite foods. If this sounds like the plan you've been looking for, read on, then put the theory into practice and take a giant step forwards towards the body you've always wanted.

7 WAYS TO EAT FOR A BIGGER AND LEANER BODY

Follow these food rules to transform your body in just eight weeks

1 FOLLOW THE 90% NUTRITION RULE

We've created the 90% Nutrition guide to make it incredibly easy for you to eat for a more muscular and leaner body without giving up all the foods you love. This guide is fully explained on p144, but following it couldn't be any simpler: all you have to do is eat to support your better-body ambitions 90% of the time, which means basing meals primarily around lean protein and veg, with some carbs and some fats (how much of each you need depends on your goal, and we'll explain more shortly).

That leaves up to 10% of your meals where you can eat for pure pleasure, including all your favourite foods and snacks, so you never suffer those motivation-zapping cravings. The 90% Nutrition guide makes eating for a bigger, stronger and leaner body so easy you'll be amazed.

2 EAT PROTEIN WITH EVERY MEAL

If you follow our Perfect Portion approach to meal-building, which is the very best way to eat for a better body and is fully explained on p152, you will eat at least a palm-sized serving of protein with every meal.

Why is eating enough protein so important to your body transformation aspirations? Lifting weights breaks down your muscle tissue, and your body needs protein to repair and rebuild your damaged muscles so they grow back bigger and stronger. Lean protein is also low in calories but rich in some of the essential vitamins and minerals that your body needs to look and perform better, and because protein takes longer to digest than carbs or fats it keeps you feeling fuller for longer so you don't get hungry between meals (and your body burns more calories digesting protein that other macronutrients).

3 BUY GOOD-QUALITY MEAT

Try to eat more free range and organic meat, fish and dairy products rather than processed products if you can afford it. It's an investment in both your short-term better-body goal and your longer-term health. Free range animals have a more varied diet and get a lot more exercise, allowing the development of more muscle, which tends to contain more vitamins A, B and K, amino acids, iron, selenium, phosphorus and zinc.

For example, beef from free range grass-fed cows tends to have much higher levels of conjugated linoleic acid and omega-3s, both types of fatty acids linked to reducing body fat levels and improving brain health, than factory-farmed and intensively reared cattle. Eating free range feels less like a frivolous luxury if you think of it this way: it's so nutritionally dissimilar to cage-reared that it's basically different food.

4 DON'T FEAR FAT

Eating fat doesn't not make you fat. Indeed, you need to consume good-quality fats if you want to build muscle and burn body fat because this macronutrient plays a number of roles in energy expenditure, vitamin storage and making testosterone, the male sex hormone. So there's no need to avoid the fats found in red meat, avocado and nuts, but do avoid hydrogenated and trans fats, which are those found in cakes, biscuits and other processed foods, because not only will they derail your muscle-building and fat-loss mission, they are also really bad for you.

Most meals in the fat-loss plan in this book have a thumb-sized serving of fats, while some of the muscle-building meals have extra portions to provide the additional calories you need to gain muscular size. But again, don't worry too much: just be guided by your hand size and don't overcomplicate it!

5 CLEAN UP YOUR CUPBOARDS

Almost all the food you put in your shopping basket (and yes, carry a basket rather than pushing a trolley) for the next eight weeks should be in its natural form or as close as possible to how its found in nature. That means stocking your fridge with plenty of lean red and white meat, fish, eggs, and as many varieties and colours of veg as you can get your hands on.

You probably know from experience that going to the supermarket when hungry always results in your trolley getting loaded with foods and snacks that are high in sugar and calories but low in the essential nutrients your body needs to get and stay lean. So only ever shop when you've recently eaten, or do a big online shop once a week so you only buy the healthier foods you know you need.

6 ALWAYS SNACK SMARTER

When you're trying to lose fat but hunger strikes between meals, always snack on low-calorie, high-satiety foods: it's much harder, for instance, to overeat carrot sticks and hummus than it is to go overboard on sweets. If you have healthy snacks to hand that will accelerate your fat-loss mission rather than derail it, this can play a huge part in how successful you are, and a little planning goes a long way to prevent you ending up glassy-eyed in front of a vending machine. And if you're aiming to add muscular size quickly it makes sense to keep high-calorie, easy-to-eat foods on hand for those days when you simply can't get in enough food via meat and veg alone. Keep a jar of nut butter, a packet of mixed nuts and pots of Greek yogurt to hand.

7 KEEP A FOOD DIARY

If you are really struggling to stay on top of your diet, even when following our 90% Nutrition guide and Perfect Portion approach, start writing a food diary. You don't need to write down every single calorie you consume, or even the number of grams of protein you've eaten. A simple note of what you ate and roughly how much of it, using your hands as the approximate guide, as well as notes on how you feel – especially your energy and motivation levels – will give you a good steer on where you are going right or what you might be doing wrong. If you're struggling to recover from workouts or feeling sluggish, for instance, you may discover that you just aren't eating enough. Even if you are feeling great with your eating plan a food diary can still be well worth keeping, because it will give you a greater insight into how certain foods make you feel and perform.

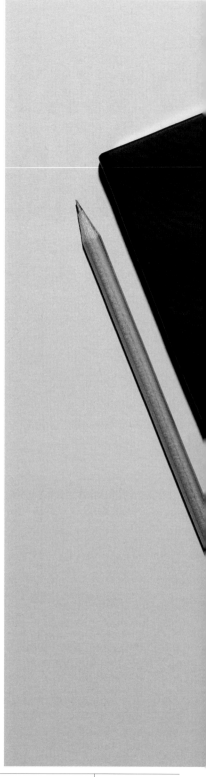

A simple note of what you ate and roughly how much of it will give you a good steer on where you are going right or what you might be doing wrong

EAT SMARTER TO BUILD A BETTER BODY

Follow our 90% Nutrition guide to burn fat fast and build muscle quickly

When it comes to whether or not you succeed in your ambition to build a bigger, stronger and leaner body, your results will ultimately be determined by the application of a single word – consistency. That means being consistent in following the eight-week training plan and, as importantly, being consistent with eating the right foods at the right time to fuel your workouts and give your body all the essential nutrients it needs to burn fat, build muscle and make you look and feel great. To help you make that happen we've created the 90% Nutrition guide to make eating for a better body easier than ever.

Most people do best when chasing a short-term body transformation goal by eating well 90% of the time and eating for pleasure the other 10% of the time

CONSISTENCY IS KING

In both scientific research and real life, consistency is what ultimately helps people control their calorie intake and manage hunger comfortably. By "comfortably" we mean causing the least amount of tension or frustration between your body composition goals (reducing your body-fat levels while increasing your lean muscle mass) and living the positive, balanced and happy life you want.

Our 90% Nutrition guide means you don't need to eat "perfectly" 100% of the time for the next eight weeks to transform your physique. And our smart eating approach means that you don't have to give up all your favourite foods, count calories, or drive yourself mad or miserable with cravings for a little bit of what you fancy.

In fact, most people do best when chasing a short-term body transformation goal by eating well 90% of the time – which means choosing nutrient-dense whole foods that will help them burn fat and build muscle – and eating for pleasure the other 10% of the time. This means you can still enjoy treats and snacks but in moderation.

Of course, if you are fully committed to achieving the very best body composition transformation possible, you will get superior results by eating for that goal 100% of the time over the next eight weeks. But if trying to maintain that 100% approach means that after a week or two you have a major blow-out and binge on foods you've been denying yourself, it's better to be consistent at 90% and allow for the odd indulgence when you fancy it.

Remember, the "all or nothing" approach rarely gets you all – it usually gets you nothing!

The 90% Nutrition guide removes all the pressure of you trying to be "perfect" with your diet all day, every day and, crucially, it allows you to eat for pure pleasure 10% of the time, to keep any cravings well and truly in check.

RETHINKING YOUR FOOD

Allowing yourself to eat for pleasure means foods are no longer categorised as either "good" or "bad". Such a black-and-white approach "moralises" foods and makes you think about certain foods in terms of guilt and regret instead of contentment and joy. That's no way to live your life if you're seeking greater health and happiness. Instead of "good" or "bad" foods, think instead of foods falling on a spectrum of "eat more often" and "eat less often". Minimally processed foods such as lean protein, vegetables, fruits, wholegrains and healthy fats are foods to eat more often. However, as we mentioned, this doesn't mean "eat always".

Highly processed foods and drinks such as chips, crisps, biscuits, cakes, pizza, bacon, ice cream, chocolate, fizzy drinks and alcohol should be consumed less often. But, again, this doesn't mean "never". Thinking about food in these terms, and then using our Perfect Portion meal-building approach (which is explained in full on p152), makes it incredibly easy to choose "eat more often" foods, while also making those "eat less often" foods a more enjoyable and guilt-free experience when you do consume them. And who doesn't want that?

KEEPING FOOD FLEXIBLE

One big advantage of 90% Nutrition is that if you're going to a wedding, party, work conference or other event where the food is likely to be in the "eat less often" category, it's not a problem! Use it as an opportunity to enjoy, in reasonable amounts, some of those foods that are good for the soul. You'll enjoy these foods guilt-free, have a fun and relaxing social experience – and still be moving towards your better body goal.

Of course, if you don't follow the 90% Nutrition approach with purpose and awareness, then it can become very easy to find yourself on a slippery slope where it's tempting to justify and rationalise consuming a higher proportion of "eat less often" foods at the expense of "eat more often" foods. To prevent this happening you need to be honest with yourself, and recognise that consistency is what really matters. If you get this right, you can follow this approach and get great results both over the next eight weeks, and then maintain your better body easily – and indefinitely.

WHAT'S IN YOUR FOOD?

Here's a guide to the major and minor components in the food you eat – and why they're so important

Every single thing we eat is a combination of different compounds. Most natural, unprocessed food consists primarily of water: a banana is 75% water, a potato is 79% water and a chicken breast, which most people think of as pure protein, can be up to 75% water. But this isn't actually that surprising when you consider you are around 70% water – so you're more H_2O than anything else!

After water the next most common compound in natural foods will be a macronutrient – there are three of them – or a combination of macronutrients along with certain micronutrients. Turn the page to find out more.

WHAT ARE MACRONUTRIENTS?

Macronutrients are the three main groups of chemical compounds that make up the food we eat. They are protein, fats and carbohydrates.

WHAT ARE MICRONUTRIENTS?

Micronutrients are chemical compounds such as vitamins, minerals and phytonutrients (plant-based nutrients) in food. They are found in much smaller quantities than macronutrients, and we only need them in very small amounts.

MACRONUTRIENT

PROTEIN

After water, most of what makes you, well, *you* is made from proteins, and all proteins are made from amino acids. There are many types of amino acid, most of which your body can manufacture itself when required, but there are nine amino acids your body can't synthesise. They're called "essential amino acids" and you must get them from food. Most foods contain at least small (or "trace") amounts of protein, but these are some of the most protein-rich foods.

ANIMAL SOURCES

- Poultry (chicken, turkey, duck, goose) and eggs
- Red meat (beef, pork, lamb)
- Wild game (venison, rabbit, pheasant)
- Fish and shellfish
- Dairy (milk, cheese, yogurt)

PLANT SOURCES

- Beans and legumes
- Tofu, tempeh and other soy products
- Nuts and seeds (though these are generally much higher in fat than protein)
- Some grains such as quinoa, amaranth and wild rice (though these are much higher in carbohydrates than protein)

HOW MUCH DO I NEED?

A good target is about 0.8g-1g of protein per kilogram of bodyweight per day, but you may need more if you're active, older, pregnant or breastfeeding, or ill or injured.

CARBOHYDRATES

There are many types of carbohydrates and they're mainly found in plant-based foods. Some carbs are very simple molecules, such as sugars, which are the most basic form. Others are much more complicated and are called complex carbohydrates. Starches, which are found in potatoes and beans, are one type of complex carb, as is fibre.

The more "simple" the carbohydrate, the easier it is to digest and absorb. In general, when eating for better health and fitness you want to prioritise consuming complex carbs because they are slower-digesting and more nutrient-rich than simple carbs.

Our bodies can't completely break down some types of complex carbs, such as insoluble fibre or resistant starch, but the bacteria in our gut love it and make other beneficial compounds from it. Fibre and resistant starch are often known as "prebiotics": they're food sources that nourish our "good" gut bacteria. Fibre also helps move things through our intestinal tract.

Higher-fibre foods include fruits and vegetables, wholegrains, beans and legumes, and nuts and seeds, while resistant starch is found in beans, green bananas and many other plant-based foods.

WATER

Make sure you're drinking enough to stay fit and focused

We are about 70% water and can't live long without it. Regulating thirst and maintaining the balance of fluids and electrolytes are two of your body's most vital tasks. We take in water through drinking, obviously, but also through eating fluid-rich fruits and veg, and we lose it through breathing, sweating and excretion.

You've probably heard you need to drink eight glasses of water per day, but there's no evidence to support that. There's also no reason for urine to be clear; a light yellow colour is fine.

There are simple ways to avoid dehydration: drink a big glass of water as soon as you wake up; pay more attention to thirst; drink more during exercise or in hot or humid conditions; choose water as your go-to drink (instead of alcohol or caffeinated drinks); and check your urine colour (the darker it is, the more dehydrated you are). If you often forget to drink enough water – you may notice you feel mentally and physically tired – fill up a water bottle at the beginning of the day, keep it close and take a big gulp every time you look at it!

THE 3 TYPES OF FAT

Most fat sources contain more than one type of dietary fat, but these foods are particularly high in one type

SATURATED
- Butter and high-fat dairy (eg cheese)
- Most animal fats
- Coconut and coconut oil
- Egg yolk
- Cacao butter

MONO-UNSATURATED
- Avocado
- Olives and olive oil
- Peanuts
- Many types of nuts, such as pecans and almonds

POLY-UNSATURATED
- Many types of seeds, such as flax, chia, sesame and sunflower seeds
- Oily fish such as salmon, herring and mackerel

BEST SOURCES OF FIBRE AND MICRONUTRIENT-RICH CARBS
- Sweet and starchy vegetables (winter squashes, beetroot)
- Starchy tubers (potatoes, sweet potatoes, yams)
- Wholegrains (rice, wheat, oats)
- Beans and legumes
- Fruit

HOW MUCH DO I NEED?
That depends on myriad factors, including your activity levels: you need more carbs if you are physically active and/or trying to build muscle. While some people do benefit from a lower-carb diet, most people look, feel and perform better from eating at least some carbs, especially the nutrient-rich, higher-fibre types.

FATS
The main three types of dietary fat are saturated, monounsaturated and polyunsaturated (see above). They differ from one another by the number and frequency of the carbon atoms that bond them, but you don't need to worry about that! You just need to know that fats are an essential macronutrient and you need to consume them for optimal health. That's one reason why very low-fat "detox diets" make you look and feel so bad!

HOW MUCH DO I NEED?
Most people do best with 25-35% of their total daily calories coming from a wide variety of healthy fat sources. Omega-3 fatty acids, particularly EPA and DHA, are special types of fats found in oily fish, seafood and some plant sources. They can help you lose weight, boost brain function, reduce inflammation, and improve both your physical and mental health – they're all-round performers!

You may have noticed that processed cooking oils, margarine and cooking sprays don't appear here and with good reason. Most "long life" cooking oils and margarines are heavily processed and contain types of fat called "trans fats" that aren't found in nature, so your body doesn't know how to process them. Research increasingly suggests trans fats contribute to many health problems.

MICRONUTRIENTS
Vitamins and minerals come in many forms and what we think of as a "vitamin" or a "mineral" is actually a group of molecules that are chemically similar, but sufficiently different to do different jobs in the body. For example "vitamin A" is actually a family of molecules, and the carotenoid forms of vitamin A (such as beta-carotene) are water-soluble, found mainly in plants (such as carrots), and not very well absorbed by the body; while the retinoid forms of vitamin A are fat-soluble, found mostly in animal foods (such as egg yolks) and are well absorbed.

We absorb minerals such as calcium, iron and magnesium from dairy and meat better than from leafy greens, which have them in harder-to-digest forms. This is one reason why it's important to eat a wide variety of foods: each food has a unique chemical "fingerprint" of micronutrients that contributes to our good health.

You may think taking a multivitamin or multi-mineral supplement helps you avoid deficiencies, but taking more vitamin and/or mineral pills is not usually better or healthier. Instead, focus on improving the quality and variety of your food choices so that you get your vitamins and minerals in the form that nature intended.

THE PERFECT PORTION MEAL PLAN

Here's how to eat for a bigger and leaner body without counting calories

You now know that our 90% Nutrition strategy – where you eat well for a better body 90% of the time and for pure pleasure 10% of the time – is the smart, sensible and sustainable way to burn fat and build lean muscle mass fast.

And while ultimately calories do matter – because to lose weight you need to be in a "calorie deficit" so your body starts tapping into fat stores for fuel – counting the calories you consume at every single meal of every single day for weeks on end takes a huge amount of time, effort and motivation. That's time, effort and motivation that could be better spent training harder, or unwinding and relaxing to help reduce stress levels.

Let's face it, who wants to be digging out measuring cups whenever they're hungry? Or be constantly cleaning food scales? Or spending good money on apps and online services to track those calorie numbers that are almost certainly inaccurate anyway? It's no wonder so many people quit counting calories almost as soon as they start.

PERFECT PORTION PLAN

Fortunately, on the New Body Plan you don't have to worry about counting calories because there is a better and easier way to know which foods you should be eating and how much of them. It's called the Perfect Portion approach and it has been adapted from a strategy created by the nutrition experts at Precision Nutriiton (precisionnutrition.com). All you need is your own hand and the ability to count to two! The approach empowers you to know exactly which food groups should make up each of your meals, and in exactly the right amounts you need. Here's what you need to know.

WHY IT WORKS

It might seem strange at first, but using your hands to work out your perfect portion sizes makes perfect sense. First, your hands are convenient: they're by your side at work lunches, restaurants, social occasions – wherever you go, they go. Second, hands are scaled to the individual. Bigger people need more food, and tend to have bigger hands, so they get larger portions. Smaller people need less food, and tend to have smaller hands, so they get smaller portions. Third, it helps you meet your specific protein, vegetable, carb, fat and energy needs at each meal without you having to count a single calorie or weigh a single gram of food!

HOW IT WORKS

If you're moderately active, here's a great way to start using the Perfect Portion approach.

A moderately active man needs a daily intake of...

- 6-8 palms of protein-dense foods
- 6-8 fists of vegetables
- 6-8 cupped handfuls of carb-dense foods
- 6-8 thumbs of fat-dense foods

**YOUR PALM DETERMINES
YOUR PROTEIN PORTIONS**
Your palm provides
approximately 25-30g of protein

**YOUR FIST DETERMINES
YOUR VEGGIE PORTIONS**
Your fist provides about 1 serving of
vegetables (weight varies depending
on the veg!)

This makes it very easy to appropriately portion each meal. For instance, if you eat three or four meals a day, the starting point for putting together each meal would be as follows...

- 2 palms of protein-dense foods
- 2 fists of vegetables
- 2 cupped handfuls of carb-dense foods
- 2 thumbs of fat-dense foods.

The Perfect Portion approach makes eating for a better body easy. How? It enables you to control your daily calorie intake almost as accurately as calorie counting, but without all the hassle and stress of kitchen scales, apps, calculators and notebooks.

It also empowers you to be much more flexible about what you decide to eat because you can easily substitute one type of protein, carbs, fats or vegetables for another, without giving a second thought to calories!

So, you fancy a palm of steak instead of a palm of chicken or tuna or turkey? Go for it. You want a fist of carrots instead of a fist of broccoli, cauliflower or green beans? No problem. You'd prefer a cupped handful of roast potatoes instead of a cupped handful of rice? Have want you want!

It really is that simple. Every single meal you eat will be determined by what you fancy or what you're craving. Not only can you say goodbye to calorie counting, you can also wave goodbye to rigid and restrictive meal plans that dictate exactly what you have to eat and when you have to eat it. That's not a sustainable approach. This is. Which is why eating for a bigger, stronger and leaner body has never been so easy.

Over the coming pages you'll discover how you can use the Perfect Portion approach to lose body fat and gain muscle, and also how to personalise the approach to help you achieve your own body transformation goals even faster.

YOUR CUPPED HAND DETERMINES YOUR CARB PORTIONS

Your cupped hand provides approximately 25-30g of carbs

YOUR THUMB DETERMINE YOUR FAT PORTIONS

Your thumb provides approximately 10-12g of fat

PERSONALISING THE PERFECT PORTION PLAN

Achieve your body composition goal faster with some smart tweaks to our better-eating guide

The Perfect Portion approach to meals is a fantastic way to eat for better health and happiness because it does away with counting calories and categorising foods as either "good" or "bad". But that's not all it does. Another big advantage of this approach is that it allows you to make adjustments to your portions easily to make them even better suited to your goals. Turn the page to find out how to do this and start benefiting from the Perfect Portion plan.

GET PERSONAL WITH THE PERFECT PORTION APPROACH

You know the basics – now use that knowledge to create a smart plan that's specific to you and your goals

It's important to remember that our portion recommendations are starting points to help you easily meet your protein, vegetable, carb, fat and energy needs without any stress or pressure – and that adjusting your portions couldn't be easier. Here's how you can do just that based on your goals.

• **Men who want to lose body fat might need to remove 2–4 cupped handfuls of carbs and/or 2–4 thumbs of fats from their daily intake**

• **Men who want to gain lean mass might need to add 2–6 cupped handfuls of carbs and/or 2–6 thumbs of fats to their daily intake**

GET PERSONAL

With these adjustments we have moved beyond starting points to a plan that's more tailored towards your primary goal. However, you can still adjust your portion sizes based on your progress. So, if you're not losing fat fast enough, remove more carb and/or fat portions. Or if you're not gaining muscle quickly enough, add more carb and/or fat portions. Reassess your results and progress every week or two, and keep making those tweaks!

EXAMPLE MENUS

Knowing you should eat a palm of protein and a fist of vegetables at every meal is great, but what does this actually look like? To give a clearer indication, here's three example daily menus based on different body composition goals. There's even some estimated nutrition data, although you should not worry about these numbers! They are there simply to show you that the hand-sized portion guidelines has taken care of them for you.

Remember these are just examples. Your actual portion sizes will depend on the size of your hand and your results. You'll notice that the fat-loss menu has a cupped handful of carbs and/or a thumb of fats removed from some meals, and the muscle-gain menu has a cupped handful of carbs and/or a thumb of fats added to some meals. Again, these are just examples and you may need to adjust them to get the results you want.

FAT-LOSS MEAL PLAN

For men wanting to lose body fat fast

BREAKFAST
2 palm-sized portions of whole eggs (~4 eggs)
2 fist-sized portions of mixed peppers and onions (~2 cups)
1 cupped handful of cooked rolled oats (~2/3 cup)
1 cupped handful of mixed berries (~2/3 cup)
1 thumb of chopped walnuts (~1tbsp)
Water/green tea/black coffee

LUNCH
2 palm-sized portions of chicken (~225g)
2 fist-sized portions of mixed greens, chopped carrots and cucumbers (~2 cups)
1 cupped handful of black beans (~2/3 cup)
1 thumb of guacamole (~1tbsp)
Water/green tea/black coffee

POST-WORKOUT SHAKE
1 palm-sized portion of chocolate protein (1 scoop)
1 cupped handful of sweet dark cherries (~2/3 cup)
1 thumb of almonds (~1tbsp)
170ml unsweetened vanilla almond milk
Ice cubes as desired

DINNER
2 palm-sized portions of wild salmon (~225g)
2 fist-sized portions of courgette (~2 cups)
1 cupped handful of sweet potato (~1 medium)
1 thumb of extra virgin olive oil (~1tbsp)
1 thumb of butter (~1tbsp)
Water

ESTIMATED NUTRITION FIGURES
Protein 185g (35% of total daily calories)
Carbs 160g (30%)
Fats 80g (35%)
Calories 2,100

MUSCLE-BUILDING MEAL PLAN

For men wanting to build muscle mass fast

BREAKFAST
1 palm-sized portion of whole eggs (~2 eggs)
1 palm-sized portion of chicken sausage (~1 sausage)
2 fist-sized portions of spinach (~2 cups)
2 cupped handfuls of wholegrain toast (~2 slices)
1 cupped handful of banana (1 medium)
2 thumbs of peanut butter (~2 thumbs)
Water/green tea/black coffee

LUNCH
2 palm-sized portions of chicken (~225g)
2 fist-sized portions of mixed peppers and onions (~2 cups)
1 cupped handful of black beans (~2/3 cup)
2 cupped handfuls of cooked brown and wild rice (~1⅓ cups)
2 thumbs of guacamole (~2tbsp)
Water/green tea/black coffee

POST-WORKOUT SHAKE
2 palm-sized portions of strawberry protein (2 scoops)
1 cupped handful of banana (~1 medium)
1 cupped handful of blueberries (~2/3 cup)
3 thumbs of almonds (~3tbsp)
340ml unsweetened vanilla almond milk
Ice cubes as desired

DINNER
2 palm-sized portions of pork (~225g)
2 fist-sized portions of green beans (~2 cups)
2 cupped handfuls of cooked quinoa (~1⅓ cups)
2 thumbs of extra virgin olive oil (~2tbsp)
Water

ESTIMATED NUTRITION FIGURES
Protein 255g (31%)
Carbs 305g (37%)
Fats 115g (32%)
Calories 3,275

MAINTENANCE MEAL PLAN

For men wanting to improve health, performance and body composition

BREAKFAST
2 palm-sized portions of whole eggs (~4 eggs)
2 fist-sized portions of broccoli, chopped (~2 cups)
1 cupped handful of cooked rolled oats (~⅔ cup)
1 cupped handful of mixed berries (~⅔ cup)
2 thumbs of slivered almonds (~2tbsp)
Water/green tea/black coffee

LUNCH
2 palm-sized portions of chicken (~225g)
2 fist-sized portions of mixed peppers and onions, cooked (~2 cups)
1 cupped handful of black beans (~⅔ cup)
1 cupped handful of cooked brown and wild rice (~⅔ cup)
2 thumbs of guacamole (~2tbsp)
Water/green tea/black coffee

POST-WORKOUT SHAKE
1 palm-sized portions of strawberry protein (1 scoop)
1 cupped handfuls of frozen mixed berries (~⅔ cup)
1 thumb of walnuts (~1tbsp)
170ml unsweetened vanilla almond milk
Ice cubes as desired

DINNER
2 palm-sized portions of lean sirloin steak (~225g)
2 fist-sized portions of asparagus (~2 cups)
2 cupped handfuls of potato (~1 large)
1 thumb of extra virgin olive oil (~1tbsp)
1 thumb of butter (~1tbsp)
Water

ESTIMATED NUTRITION FIGURES
Protein 200g (32%)
Carbs 230g (37%)
Fats 85g (31%)
Calories: 2,485

YOU AND YOUR GUT

The gut is known as your "second brain" with good reason, and taking better care of it will pay big health and happiness rewards

The old saying goes that "you are what you eat". But a more accurate version would be "you are what you absorb". The food you eat has an enormous effect on your health and well-being, from how easily you lose or gain weight to your risk of certain illnesses and diseases. What is not so well understood, but just as important, is the impact of *how* you eat and how this affects nutrient absorption.

Research shows listening to different types of music, eating from coloured plates and even the weight of cutlery can all affect the speed and amount you eat, as well as your meal enjoyment. But it's not just external factors at play: the digestive system is highly sensitive to signals coming from your brain, and your physiological and psychological state at mealtimes has a significant impact on how well you digest food and absorb nutrients.

CHRONIC STRESS

While we no longer face that "quick, run, there's a tiger!" type of acute stress, many of us suffer from long-term, or chronic, stress that seems an inevitable part of modern life (it's not inevitable, and exercising and eating well are two of the best ways to reduce stress).

Chronic stress is really bad for your health. It depletes essential nutrients and impairs the body's repair, growth and recovery processes; it causes more of what you eat to be poorly digested; and it can create impairments in the gut that trigger allergies, bloating and autoimmune disorders such as IBS.

It also diverts our attention and energy to what's stressing us and away from more beneficial activities. Prolonged periods of stress can drive us to use food as a distraction or escape, and you're less likely to be aware of what and how much you're eating, increasing the chances of overeating and making matters worse.

THE DIGESTION PROCESS

The digestive system is composed of the mouth, oesophagus, stomach, small intestine, large intestine (or gut) and rectum. Digestion starts in the mouth, with the enzymes in your saliva that begin to break down food, but most of the action occurs in your stomach.

That's where enzymes reduce the larger pieces of food into smaller components. Proteases break down proteins into amino acids; amylases break down carbs into simple sugars; and lipases break down fats into fatty acids.

These nutrients are then absorbed through the wall of the small intestine into the bloodstream where they travel through the circulatory system until they get to where they're needed. Any nutrients that aren't immediately needed are stored or excreted.

STRESS AND DIGESTION

You've probably heard of the "fight, flight or freeze" response, which is how the body responds to danger to give it the best chance of survival, known scientifically as the sympathetic nervous system. We also have the parasympathetic nervous system, which is the "rest and digest" side to the system.

These two parts of the nervous system work like traffic lights: when one system is "on" or green, the other is "off" or red. They can't both be green at the same time (otherwise there'll be chaos).

What's this got to do with eating and your gut? A lot, actually! Because the two systems can't run simultaneously, that means when you're stressed it is very difficult to digest food properly. Your appetite is suppressed, the movement of food through your digestive system slows, and blood flow is directed away from your digestive tract to your limbs to help you escape or fight off the perceived danger.

QUICK TIP

Your gut and your brain are very closely linked and your digestive system shuts down when you're stressed. Eating in a stressed state reduces how well your body is able to digest the food you eat and absorb nutrients from it, increases the risk of overeating and weight gain, and isn't enjoyable – in short, it sucks! The good news is that there's an antidote to stressful eating and it can make you leaner and happier! Turn the page to discover more about mindful eating.

MEALTIME MINDFULNESS

Here's why being more "present" when you eat can make you bigger and leaner

We've mentioned "mindfulness" and "mindful eating" briefly already, so here's what it means and why being mindful during meals makes a big difference to your body composition, and your health and happiness.

Mindfulness is simply the practice of paying attention (in a non-judgemental way) to an activity. It's a very effective method to manage stress: one study found regular mindfulness meditation actually changes the structure of the brain, creating more neural connections, which might protect us from depression and dementia.

Ultimately, being more mindful gives you a different perspective on your thoughts and feelings and helps you approach situations in a calmer, more thoughtful way. And being mindful when eating can have a positive impact on your physical and mental health, without requiring too much effort.

- *Take the bite and chew slowly, noticing the different flavours and textures and how they change as you chew.*
- *Put down your cutlery. This helps you focus on swallowing this mouthful before starting the next.*
- *After you swallow, be aware of the food moving to your stomach and how it affects your level of hunger.*

THE MINDFULNESS CONNECTION

When you eat mindfully you pay attention to the appearance, texture and taste of your food, and your body's hunger signals. It takes time for your brain to register signals from your stomach's stretch receptors, so mindful eating can prevent overeating by slowing you down and making you more aware of how you're feeling (regularly overeating can blunt your body's fullness signals and contribute to weight gain). Mindfulness can also enhance the pleasure you derive from food, so you're less likely to overeat because you've taken time to really enjoy your meal.

Being more mindful also makes it easier to eat a wider variety of foods, and being non-judgemental makes you open to trying new foods. This is important because you might be missing out on something you'll really like, and the more varied your diet the lower your risk of any nutrient deficiencies.

EAT MINDFULLY TO BUILD MUSCLE!

You don't need any special equipment or apps to begin mindful eating – in fact, the fewer distractions you have the better! Here's how to get started:

1 Turn off the TV and put away your phone. We're so used to watching or reading while eating that this might feel difficult at first, so really focus on the colours and smells on your plate.

2 Sit at a table. This will help you focus on the food in front of you and emphasises that mealtimes are an important activity, not a chore to be squeezed in where possible.

3 Start small. Being mindful at mealtimes takes time and practice and you will get distracted. Begin by aiming to take just one mindful mouthful per meal. Here's how:

- *Take a moment to look at the food on the plate, noticing the smells, colours and textures.*
- *Pick up a forkful or spoonful and take a moment to notice the qualities of the food.*

If you are new to mindful eating you can continue eating in this way, or return to your old eating habits. But do try to add in an extra mindful mouthful each day until you eat a full mindful meal.

Just one mindful meal or snack a day will improve your relationship with food and help you listen to and understand your body better.

QUICK TIP

Eating when distracted reduces your enjoyment of food and increases the risk of overeating and emotional eating. But practising slow, mindful eating, chewing every mouthful properly, will heighten your enjoyment of food, improve digestion and help prevent overeating.

GET SMART WITH SUPPLEMENTS

Use the right sports nutrition products
to burn fat and build muscle faster

If you've ever had an isotonic drink after playing sport, a protein shake after the gym, or popped a daily multivitamin pill, then you have taken a supplement or a sports nutrition product. While they aren't magic pills – exercise, eating and sleeping are the three big-picture pieces in any better-body attempt – supplements can make a positive difference to how you look and feel by providing your body with all the essential vitamins, minerals and other micronutrients it needs to build muscle, burn fat and function optimally.

So think of supplements as an insurance policy to fill in any nutritional gaps that are difficult or impossible to cover with your daily diet. Here are ten supplements – all fully supported by science – that you may want to consider taking to accelerate your progress towards a bigger, stronger and leaner body.

WHEY PROTEIN POWDER

WHAT IS IT?

Whey is a by-product of the cheese-making process – the liquid left over once the milk has been curdled and strained. In its powdered form. whey protein is one of the most popular sports nutrition products in the world because it's very rapidly digested, which means it gets to your muscles very quickly after training to kick-start muscle protein synthesis (MPS) – the process of repairing muscle damage caused by training to make your muscles bigger and stronger.

DO I NEED IT?

If you are following the New Body Plan training programme to the letter – as you should be if you are serious about making positive changes to your body – then you should invest in a tub of high-quality whey powder. A whey protein shake, ideally made with cold water or skimmed milk, taken within 30 minutes of the end of your training session will flood your bloodstream with amino acids (the building blocks of protein), which are quickly shuttled into your muscle cells where they are laid down as new muscle tissue.

OMEGA-3 FISH OIL

WHAT IS IT?

Omega-3 is an essential fatty acid, which means that our bodies can't manufacture it so we need to consume it from our diet. It is found in high concentrations in oily fish, especially those that live in colder waters. Omega-3 is very important for healthy metabolic function and adequate intake provides a whole host of other health benefits, including reducing the risk of cardiovascular disease, certain cancers, mental health disorders and inflammation.

DO I NEED IT?

The consumption of fish is a very important component of a healthy and balanced diet. If you're not getting the recommended two portions of fish per week, one white and one oily (and the chances are you're not because the UK average is only a third of a portion per week), then you should consider supplementation. And in case you were wondering, a fish fillet covered in batter alongside a huge pile of thick chips and mushy peas isn't the right option to increase your intake of omega-3 if you want to burn off as much body fat as possible.

PRE-WORKOUTS

WHAT IS IT?

Designed to be taken ahead of your training session, pre-workout supplements contain a combination of compounds intended to improve focus, performance and energy, as well as better blood flow to deliver oxygen and nutrients to your working muscles faster. The key ingredients typically include caffeine, the amino acids beta-alanine and arginine, and creatine, but it may also contain other compounds.

DO I NEED IT?

Research supports claims that caffeine improves focus and concentration, and many people say they get a superior "pump" because of increased blood flow to the working muscles. For some, taking a pre-workout formula also provides a psychological boost that gets them fired up for their session and so they consequently perform better. However, the jury is still out on whether some of the ingredients provide some of the reported performance benefits, such as limiting lactic acid build-up to prevent cramp. And you should always test a small sample of a product before taking a full dose to make sure you don't suffer any adverse reactions.

VITAMIN D

WHAT IS IT?

Vitamin D is a fat-soluble vitamin-like compound that plays an essential role in a huge number of biological functions, as well as improving cognition and reducing the risk of certain cancers, cardiovascular disease and dementia. It is produced by your body when your skin is exposed to direct sunlight, but is also found in low doses in some foods, such as fish and eggs.

DO I NEED IT?

If you live in the UK, or other higher-latitude parts of the northern hemisphere, then the chances are that you will have some level of vitamin D deficiency. One study found more than 50% of the UK adult population have sub-optimal levels because there isn't enough strong sunlight for much of the year to make production possible.

BCAAs

WHAT IS IT?

A combined form of three of the nine essential amino acids – leucine, isoleucine and valine. They are called "essential" because your body can't manufacture them and so they must be obtained through the food you eat.

DO I NEED IT?

Research is fairly conclusive that BCAA supplementation before, during and after training can help induce muscle protein synthesis, which is the technical term for the process that lays down new muscle tissue so your muscles grow bigger and stronger. BCAAs also improve muscular endurance, increase energy levels, and reduce

SHOULD I TAKE SUPPLEMENTS EVERY DAY?

It all depends on the product you're taking. Some supplements are meant to be taken daily, such as multivitamins and fish oil, because they are proven to improve general health and well-being. Others, such as whey protein powder, can also be taken on non-training days as a quick and easy way to increase your daily protein intake. Pre-workout formulas should be only taken immediately before training. If you are in any doubt about when or how often you should take a certain product, simply check the product's label or company website for guidance.

recovery time. High use of BCAAs can deplete levels of other nutrients, especially vitamin B6, so either choose a product that also contains this B vitamin, or take a daily a multivitamin.

CREATINE

WHAT IS IT?

Creatine is an organic compound that exists naturally in the body and is instrumental in providing energy to your cells. It is not an essential nutrient because your body can make it from two amino acids (glycine and arginine), but it can also be consumed through certain foods. Red meat, such as steak, is naturally high in creatine.

DO I NEED IT?

Even if you eat a lot of red meat, supplementing with creatine will increase your body's natural levels to provide a number of significant performance and physique benefits. Research has shown that creatine supplementation can increase physical performance, especially in successive bursts of short-term, high-intensity exercise, such as weight training or interval training, because the energy it supplies enables your muscles to work harder for longer. Always take creatine with plenty of water to avoid any risk of dehydration, and some people may benefit from taking it with food to help prevent avoid any potential stomach upset or discomfort.

CASEIN PROTEIN POWDER

WHAT IS IT?

A type of protein that takes a long time to be digested so it releases its amino acids slowly and steadily into the bloodstream, where they are "drip fed" into your muscles – unlike whey protein, which is rapidly digested and absorbed. It is found in its natural form in dairy products including cow's milk, where it constitutes up to 80% of the milk's protein content.

DO I NEED IT?

Its slow-release nature makes casein the perfect type of protein to take before bed, because it feeds your muscles slowly overnight while you sleep to assist the repair and recovery process. You can also supplement with casein protein during the day in situations when you are very busy or travelling and face extended periods between meals.

ZINC

WHAT IS IT?

Zinc is an essential trace element that's found in up to 300 different enzymes and plays a part in a huge number of biological roles, including DNA metabolism, hormone production

CAN I USE SUPPS INSTEAD OF REGULAR MEALS?

Some supplements, especially in the weight-loss sector, are promoted as meal-replacement products (MRPs). But whether your goal is reducing body fat, building lean muscle or improving general health and fitness, fresh, whole and natural food should always be your preferred nutrition option over pills, bars or shakes. These products are useful in situations where you have no alternative other than going hungry, but always remember, they are called "supplements" for a good reason: good-quality food takes priority.

and function (including testosterone), brain health, and efficient central nervous system function, among many others. Shellfish and red meat, especially beef, lamb and liver, are among the best dietary sources of zinc.

DO I NEED IT?

There's no official UK recommended daily intake, but in the US the RDA is 11mg per day for men, yet only 58% of Americans meet this target, according to the US Department of Agriculture. Eating organic fish and red meat regularly should enable you to hit this target, and while zinc is also found in plants, increasingly poor soil quality due to over-farming means produce is now typically less nutrient-dense than a generation ago. Zinc is lost through sweat, so supplementation could be a smart move.

MAGNESIUM

WHAT IS IT?

Like zinc, magnesium is an essential trace element – every single cell in your body needs magnesium ions to function because they're involved in the production of energy, while hundreds of enzymes require its presence to work optimally. Nuts, green leafy vegetables and wholegrains are the best dietary sources.

DO I NEED IT?

The UK recommended daily intake for magnesium is 300mg for men. But with 68% of Americans not hitting their daily target, according to the US Department of Agriculture, it's likely that percentage is replicated in the UK too, given our similar diets and lifestyles. Magnesium is needed for central nervous system function and muscle contractions, both of which are a big part of training, and exercise can deplete your levels, so supplementation might be worth considering.

MULTIVITAMIN

WHAT IS IT?

Exactly what is sounds like: a tablet or capsule that contains either all or a significant dose of the recommended daily intake of all the essential micronutrients you need to function optimally.

DO I NEED IT?

If you are eating a natural and varied whole-food diet then you should get all the vitamins and minerals you need. However, mass-produced factory foods dominate our supermarket aisles, and soil and air pollution and increasing pesticide use means that many foods now have lower levels of nutrients than at any time in history. Popping a daily multivitamin can act as a good insurance policy to ensure you hit your daily target of essential nutrients.

CONTINUE BUILDING A BIGGER AND LEANER BODY!

Your eight-week New Body Plan transformation journey may be over, but you can still keep making big changes to the way you look and feel

You may have finished your eight-week journey towards a better body with a photoshoot, allowing you to record that impressive "after" shot that you can proudly display in contrast to that "before" picture – the picture that, when you look at it now, feels like a distant memory or even an image of a completely different person from the man you are today. Or you may have capped your transformation with a wedding, a holiday or another big life event that was the reason you started the plan.

However you end your challenge, what you do in the days and week after your last session have a huge impact on for how long you can maintain your bigger and leaner body, and some simple steps can even help you continue making lean muscle mass gains. Here's how!

TOAST YOUR TRANSFORMATION

Once that final session is in the bag, or the final photographs are taken, it can be tempting to go wild and reward your efforts with pizza, burgers, beers or whatever else you've had to cut back on for the last two months. While toasting your transformation is no bad thing – indeed a big intake of carbs and calories may actually make you look bigger and leaner the following day as your muscles refill their depleted cells with energy – suddenly going from training hard and eating well to no exercise and eating everything in sight will undo some of your positive body composition changes quite quickly. Besides, after eight weeks of smart training and sensible eating, you're going to look and feel great, and you'll probably be far more inclined to keep going on your journey than jack it all in and return to your old ways.

ONWARDS AND UPWARDS

If you haven't yet signed up at **newbodyplan.co.uk** do so now to get a wealth of expert lifestyle advice, training tips and eating ideas sent straight to your inbox, so you can keep making big improvements to how you look without a top on.

As mentioned, eating more food, especially high-quality produce, can make you look bigger and leaner in the days after the end of your challenge. For instance, if you've been following the Perfect Portion approach of the fat-loss meal plan, try transitioning to the muscle-building guidelines – which include more servings of carbs and fats per day. That's a great way to gradually increase your daily calorie intake and give your body more of the nutrients it needs to add new muscle mass without gaining body fat.

Alternatively, if you've been following the muscle-building meal plan and are happy with your new size but now want to cut some remaining body fat, using the fat-loss meal plan approach to reduce your daily calorie intake is the smart decision. Another option is to use your new-found knowledge of eating for a better body to devise your own unique approach to nutrition that fits perfectly with your life and training goals. That will keep you on the right track for a bigger, stronger and leaner body.

As for your training, you have plenty of options! You could go back to the start of the plan and do it again, but this time using heavier weights because you're now far stronger and fitter. Or you could do one of the specific blocks, depending on whether you want to prioritise getting really strong, much more muscular or super-ripped. But do check out **newbodyplan.co.uk** to discover our bespoke workout plans to take your better-body aspirations onwards and upwards!

YOUR TOTAL BODY TRANSFORMATION GUIDE!

NEW BODY PLAN

Lose fat and add muscle in just eight weeks!

We'd love to hear about your New Body Plan journey towards a bigger, leaner and stronger body. Share your story with us using #NewBodyPlan

@NewBodyPlan

newbodyplan.co.uk

@NewBodyPlan